CHAPTER ONE
PLACES TO EAT

Silo

RESTAURANT | BRIGHTON | BN1 4AN

Silo is a bakery, coffee house and restaurant, serving delicious, healthy food in a calm and relaxed atmosphere. Easy on the eye, with simple décor and a rustic feel , fans of Silo love the airy, spacious layout. Thanks to the open plan kitchen you can watch your food being prepared in front of you.

Silo is focused around a zero waste policy. They eliminate waste by opting for re-usable delivery vessels and sourcing local ingredients that produce no waste. Silo is a great example of an independent business that not only cares about its customers, but also works hard to care for the environment.

ADDRESS
No39 Upper Gardner Street
BN1 4AN

PHONE
01273 674259

WEBSITE
bestofengland.com/001

64 Degrees

RESTAURANT | BRIGHTON | BN1 1HB

64 Degrees is a small restaurant tucked away in the Brighton Lanes, but don't let the size fool you. This amazing eatery has won multiple awards including Best Restaurant at the Brighton & Hove Food Awards 2014 and a Bib Gourmand by Michelin - all thanks to passionate chefs and on the ball serving staff.

The décor inside 64 Degrees has a modern, pared-back feel, with an open plan kitchen. The layout really brings together all the best components of a successful restaurant, allowing you insights into how their tasty menu is created, as well as bringing an exciting atmosphere to the fine dining experience.

ADDRESS
53 Meeting House Ln, Brighton
BN1 1HB

PHONE
01273 770115

WEBSITE
bestofengland.com/002

The Curlew

RESTAURANT | BODIAM | TN32 5UY

Formerly a 17th century coaching inn, today The Curlew in Bodiam is a relaxed, informal restaurant boasting a refined, modern British menu. The interior is smart with additional dining during the summer on their sunny garden terrace, surrounded by planters filled with herbs and edible flowers.

Created by Mark and Sara Colley, The Curlew is in its 8th year. Diners can expect dishes such as their highly esteemed Sussex farmhouse soufflé, and locally reared sirloin of beef with glazed tongue. For dessert how about treacle tart with peach and lemon thyme, accompanied by Earl Grey ice cream?

ADDRESS
Junction Rd, Bodiam
TN32 5UY

PHONE
01580 861394

WEBSITE
bestofengland.com/003

Fatto A Mano

RESTAURANT | BRIGHTON | BN1 4JF

Pizza and Italian bites don't get better than this. Fatto a Mano is an authentic Italian neighbourhood restaurant, minutes from central Brighton. What's so special? They use the highest quality ingredients and keep things simple - no weird pizza toppings, just authentic Italian flavours. It's a great fun place too.

Soak up the atmosphere and enjoy a memorable dining experience, suitable for families and couples alike. We recommend sitting at the bar where you might learn a word or two of Italian as the staff are largely Italian, and many of the diners come for a taste of home too. Don't forget to try the Scugnizzielli.

ADDRESS
77 London Rd, Brighton
BN1 4JF

PHONE
01273 600621

WEBSITE
bestofengland.com/004

The George

RESTAURANT | RYE | TN31 7JT

The George in the heart of historic Rye combines bar, restaurant, hotel and stylish wedding venue. At the luxury end of the scale, The George has 34 bedrooms and a fine dining restaurant. This place oozes charm and is renowned for reliably good service. There's even a stunning Georgian ballroom on site.

The menu at The George is described as 'modern European with a sunny, Mediterranean slant'. We love the fact that dishes include fresh fish brought in from the trawlers of Rye Bay as well as locally sourced meats. Full English breakfasts and afternoon teas are also served here, in a uniquely English setting.

ADDRESS
98 High Street, Rye
TN31 7JT

PHONE
01797 222114

WEBSITE
bestofengland.com/005

5

St Clements

RESTAURANT | ST LEONARDS | TN38 0EB

When chef patron Nick Hales visited the Hastings area, he soon noticed an opportunity to open a restaurant that celebrated the bountiful local produce. The ethos behind the restaurant was to mix both a pared back atmosphere and amazing food so that guests could fine dine without the frills.

Inside the restaurant there is a simple yet stylish interior with sleek furniture and contemporary art. The menu is impressive with lunch, brunch and dinner done in impeccable style. St Clements specialises in seafood with incredible dishes such as smoked haddock, chargrilled scallops and seabass.

ADDRESS
3 Mercatoria, St Leonards
TN38 0EB

PHONE
01424 200355

WEBSITE
bestofengland.com/006

The Salt Room

RESTAURANT | BRIGHTON | BN1 2FA

The Salt Room has been the talk of Brighton since the day it opened in February 2015. It's a modern seafood and meat restaurant with privileged views to Brighton's seafront, making a meal here a must if you're in town for a special occasion. Private dining is available for hire, and 'BYO Mondays' are popular.

The Salt Room is a spacious restaurant, oozing urban chic. The bar is run by very talented barmen, whose stunning cocktails set the tone for an unforgettable, dining experience. Food is innovative and service is exceptional. The seaside-inspired dessert, 'Taste of the Pier', is a visual and taste sensation.

ADDRESS

106 King's Rd, Brighton
BN1 2FA

PHONE

01273 929488

WEBSITE

bestofengland.com/011

The Loft

RESTAURANT | **ARUNDEL** | BN18 9DJ

The Loft at Sparks Yard is a California-inspired restaurant occupying the entire third floor of Sparks Yard General Store in Arundel. The space is light and modern which creates a welcoming environment. The Loft prides itself on being family friendly, and caters for vegetarian, vegan and gluten free diets.

The menu here celebrates the best of American style cuisine with irresistible favourites such as pancakes, burgers and macaroni as well as more healthy options such as superfood salads. Always thinking of the customer, the owners have provided a lift, handy baby-changing facilities, and free Wi-Fi.

ADDRESS
18 Tarrant St, Arundel
BN18 9DJ

PHONE
01903 885588

WEBSITE
bestofengland.com/014

Field and Fork

RESTAURANT | CHICHESTER | PO19 1NJ

Field & Fork is a delightful restaurant in a central but hidden away location in Chichester, West Sussex. Service is friendly but unobtrusive and the fine-dining dishes revolve around what can be sourced fresh from the market that morning. The conservatory at the rear was soaked in sunshine on our visit.

We also love the charming open log fire, and the comfortable surroundings. If you are visiting Chichester Theatre, this is an ideal stop off for a top-notch pre-theatre meal. Or if you're looking for an intimate venue for a family celebration or business lunch the restaurant is available for private hire.

ADDRESS
4 Guildhall Street, Chichester
PO19 1NJ

PHONE
01243 789915

WEBSITE
bestofengland.com/022

Drakes

RESTAURANT | BRIGHTON | BN2 1PE

For a really special treat, why not splash out on an unforgettable dining experience at Drakes, in Brighton's characterful Kemptown? The restaurant at Drakes has won multiple awards since its opening in 2004, and has been named by a prestigious magazine as the best fine dining restaurant in Brighton.

As you might expect, service is impeccable and the food is fantastic. There's an extensive wine list but if you're no wine expert, worry not, as there's a Sommelier on hand to help. Style-wise we're talking sleek and sophisticated, and it's worth dressing up for a cocktail in the plush 24-hour cocktail bar.

ADDRESS

43-44 Marine Parade,
Brighton
BN2 1PE

PHONE

01273 696934

9

bestofengland.com/008

The Leconfield

RESTAURANT | PETWORTH | GU28 0AS

The Leconfield is an award winning restaurant and bar - a classy establishment offering great food in comfortable surroundings. An outside courtyard is perfect for al fresco dining, and the glass wall along the back of the restaurant floods the room with natural light. Upstairs rooms are ideal for private dining.

The building dates from the 17th century and offers a classy, tranquil setting, and fantastic choice when it comes to the food. You can choose from the Set Menu, A La Carte Menu and the Pinchos Menu during the summer months.

ADDRESS

New Street, Petworth
GU28 0AS

PHONE

01798 345111

10

bestofengland.com/009

Coach House

RESTAURANT | BRIGHTON | BN1 1AL

This exquisite bar/restaurant is situated in the heart of the Brighton Lanes, a pebble's throw from the beach. Serving hot meals and a variety of drinks in a calm, comfortable atmosphere, this is a popular choice for visitors and locals. Enjoy the roaring winter fire and lazy summer lunches in the courtyard.

A sit down meal can be enjoyed here, as well as a chilled catch up with friends at the bar. The restaurant is open for lunch and dinner with daily specials. There is also free Wi-Fi, which means that it's a handy place to catch up on some work while having a break from busy city life.

ADDRESS

59 Middle St, Brighton
BN1 1AL

PHONE

01273 719000

11

i bestofengland.com/010

Front Room

RESTAURANT | SEAFORD | BN25 1PL

The Front Room is a popular meeting spot in Seaford, famed for its delicious coffees and cakes. Owners Victoria and Mac work hard to make this the great place it is. They're past winners of the coveted 'Café of the year in Sussex' award. The café is made up of two large rooms and has lovely outside decking.

Look out for the 'kids' corner' out the back, making this a family friendly environment. The décor is fresh and modern, bringing a new style to Seaford. On Friday night, the Front Room is transformed into a tapas restaurant, serving tapas influenced by Spanish and North African flavours.

ADDRESS

42 High St, Seaford
BN25 1PL

PHONE

01323 895383

12

i bestofengland.com/012

Tuscan Kitchen

RESTAURANT | RYE | TN31 7LB

Since opening in 2009, the Tuscan Kitchen has become one of Rye's favourites. You are always welcomed with a smile from the friendly staff, and you'll love the intimate, homely feel of the place. Food-wise, expect delicious authentic Tuscan and regional Italian cuisine, as well as a great selection of wines.

It's always worth booking as this popular eatery can get very busy. If you're in the medieval town of Rye, and manage to get a table, it's a must.

ADDRESS

8 Lion St, Rye
TN31 7LB

PHONE

01797 223269

13

 bestofengland.com/013

The Set

RESTAURANT | BRIGHTON | BN1 2GG

For stunning British tasting menus in the heart of buzzing Brighton, head to The Set. This modern restaurant is attached to the Artist Residence Hotel in centrally-positioned Regency Square. It's a hidden gem, well worth a visit, and a great place to eat whether you're a hotel resident or calling in.

The Set triples up as a bar and café, as well as a restaurant. Boasting sea views out to the iconic West Pier, pop in to chill whether you fancy an Earl Grey tea, espresso, or Pornstar Martini. We think you'll love the eclectic décor and relaxed atmosphere. The Set is quirky, cosy and totally unique.

ADDRESS

33 Regency Square,
Brighton
BN1 2GG

PHONE

01273 855572

14

 bestofengland.com/015

Tell your friends about us.

If you like our work then please tell your friends about us.

We are a small company of passionate photographers and word of mouth is the best advertising we have.

Better yet, please give them the discount code below and they will save 10% on their first order.

Discount Code:

BESTOFDISCOUNT

BEST OF ENGLAND
PASSIONATE ABOUT QUALITY

The Limetree Kitchen

LEWES | BN7 2DA | 01273 478636

A licensed restaurant in Station Street in the centre of Lewes, Limetree Kitchen's food philosophy embraces a highly creative approach to the best quality ingredients, sourced locally whenever possible. Visit for coffee and Eggs Benedict, lunches and snacks during the day, or enjoy an indulgent evening meal.

 bestofengland.com/016

281

Half Man Half Burger

ST. LEONARDS | TN38 0DX | 01424 552332

Passionate, quirky and delicious. Half Man! Half Burger! seeks to provide the folk of St.Leonards & Hastings with a unique place to enjoy top quality burgers. Travelling across the pond, the team at Half Man! Half Burger! have taken inspiration from the relaxed vibe and the generous portions found in American burger joints.

 bestofengland.com/017

15

Paulino

LINDFIELD | RH16 2HP | 01444 484 824

Paulino is a family run Italian restaurant, situated on the high street of the lovely town of Lindfield. Their popularity is no surprise as they offer a fantastic all round experience, with excellent food at great prices as well as extremely helpful and friendly staff.

 bestofengland.com/018

16

Plateau

BRIGHTON | BN1 1HG | 01273 733085

This is a charming French gem in the South Lanes, Brighton. Plateau is a wine bar and restaurant with a dynamic vibe, a relaxed décor and a passion not just for food and wine, but also for music. A handpicked wine list of the most exciting wines compliments the carefully prepared continental-inspired food.

 bestofengland.com/019

273

Food For Friends

BRIGHTON | BN1 1HF | 01273 202310

An icon in the South Lanes, Food for Friends offers the freshest seasonal ingredients in a calmly serene setting. Regulars say if you're not a vegetarian, this place might well convert you. Each dish is a work of art and innovation, so no wonder Food for Friends has won a host of awards in recent years.

 bestofengland.com/020

272

Senor Buddha

BRIGHTON | BN1 4QE | 01273 567832

Fusion cuisine has never been as exciting as this. Senor Buddha combines authentic Spanish tapas with a dramatic East Asian twist. Having travelled across Spain and Eastern Asia, owner and foodie Lee Shipley has built up his knowledge of both cuisines allowing him to combine unusual flavours to great effect.

 bestofengland.com/021

271

Butlers

ARUNDEL | BN18 9DG | 01903 882222

Butlers is a family run restaurant located in the heart of Arundel and has been serving delicious homemade food since 1995. Offering a great selection of dishes, all for a reasonable price. The atmosphere is relaxed, perfect for enjoying a drink at the bar or a sit down meal.

 bestofengland.com/023

17

Meat Liquor

BRIGHTON | BN1 4GU | 01273 917710

Meat Liquor is a fun, colourful and vibrant burger bar that's well known for its American style food and funky cocktails. The restaurant is based in the regenerated London Road area of Brighton, and is perfectly suited to the outgoing style the city has to offer. You're likely to find a younger crowd here.

 bestofengland.com/024

270

The Parsons Table

ARUNDEL BN18 9DG | 01903 883477

The Parsons Table in Arundel is dedicated to offering the very best of local and seasonal ingredients in a relaxed environment with perfect service to match. Lee Parsons has been a chef for over 20 years worldwide, alongside some of the biggest names and now can showcase his talent in his own restaurant.

 bestofengland.com/025

18

H.en

BRIGHTON | BN1 4ER | 01273 671004

H.en is a weird but wonderful little café/chicken restaurant. Here you can enjoy the meals you love but with a delicious healthy twist. The menu suits vegetarians as well, offering a popular halloumi burger. Located on Trafalgar Street, close to Brighton station, this is a handy stop off in the North Laine.

 bestofengland.com/026

269

Banyan

FERNHURST GU27 3HA | 01428 644090

It's hard to beat a curry. Banyan comes recommended as it offers authentic Indian cuisine within a charming old barn next to the King's Arms Pub in Fernhurst. Dishes to tempt you include Keralan Fish Curry and Swordfish Tikka, created by professional Indian chefs using locally sourced, fresh ingredients.

 bestofengland.com/027

62

The Coal Shed

BRIGHTON | BN1 1AN | 01273 322998

The Coal Shed is a gourmet steak and seafood restaurant in the heart of Brighton. Named as one of the best restaurants in the UK by the prestigious Observer Food Monthly Awards, it has also been recommended by The Telegraph and The Guardian, amongst others. It's important to book ahead, for obvious reasons.

 bestofengland.com/028

268

Ginger Pig

HOVE | BN3 2TR | 01273 736123

The Ginger Pig in Hove, part of the Gingerman Restaurants Group, is a welcoming, contemporary pub with a large dining area. Awarded Best Food Pub in the Brighton & Hove Food Awards for the past three years running, the Ginger Pig serves bar snacks as well as a full food menu for adults and children.

 bestofengland.com/029

267

Riddle and Finns

BRIGHTON | BN1 2FN | 01273 821218

Riddle & Finns is a much loved Brighton champagne and oyster bar, serving a large selection of high end seafood. Their fresh fish and shellfish are locally sourced from Shoreham. There are two Riddle & Finn restaurants which are based in the famous Brighton Lanes and along Brighton's seafront with wonderful sea views.

 bestofengland.com/030

266

The Wine Shed

ST. LEONARDS | TN37 6DY | 01424 420020

The Wine Shed in St.Leonards is a newcomer to the scene and a mighty welcome one. The proprietors have compiled an extensive wine list and serve a selection of tapas style small plates, and main meals to go with your vino. It's a great spot to feast on cheese boards and salads, steaks and Sunday roasts.

 bestofengland.com/031

20

Pizza Face

HOVE | BN3 5AB | 01273 965651

Pizzaface is an independent pizza business located in Hove. There's also a larger store in Kemptown. The company started in 2009 when a rundown pizzeria in Kemptown was transformed into a new and improved pizza place. The aim of the owners is to make the best quality, most flavoursome pizza possible.

 bestofengland.com/032

265

The Chilli Pickle

BRIGHTON | BN1 1GE | 01273 900383

Don't miss this bright and buzzing dining experience right in the centre of Brighton, just across the piazza from the library. The Chilli Pickle offers an original pan-Indian menu full of flavours, textures and aromas. Many of the dishes are street food-inspired and the homemade ice cream is amazing.

 bestofengland.com/033

264

Buxted Hotel

UCKFIELD | TN22 4AY | 0845 0727412

The Buxted Park Restaurant near Uckfield celebrates fine British cuisine and good quality wines. With two AA rosettes you can expect only the best in local produce and attentive service. On fine days guests can enjoy great food and a drink out in the attractive hotel grounds overlooking magnificent Buxted Park.

 bestofengland.com/034

21

Jeremy's

HAY. HEATH | RH16 1XP | 01444 441102

Jeremy's Restaurant is located a few miles north of Haywards Heath within the charming grounds of Borde Hill Gardens. The restaurant prides itself on its locally sourced ingredients. The light and airy interior has large windows with views out to the terrace. You can dine outside in the pretty walled garden.

 bestofengland.com/035

22

Richmond Arms

CHICHESTER | PO18 0QB | 01243 775537

The Richmond Arms is set on the famous Goodwood Estate and much of the excellent produce is sourced from the restaurant's affiliated organic farm, or foraged on site. The menu at The Richmond Arms is essentially British with dishes including Goodwood rack of lamb and estate-reared roast beef.

 bestofengland.com/036

23

CHAPTER TWO
Public Houses

Noah's Ark

PUBLIC HOUSE | LURGASHALL | GU28 9ET

The Noah's Ark in Lurgashall is a bewitching 16th century pub located just a stone's throw from Blackdown Hill on the borders of Surrey and West Sussex. Step inside to find a wonderful mix of old meets new - ancient fireplaces and low beams, alongside comfy leather sofas and contemporary design features.

This child-friendly pub is renowned for its seasonal food and great service, and is recommended in the Michelin and AA guides among others. The front garden of the Noah's Ark overlooks the large village green making it a wonderful place to sit during the summer months and watch the locals play cricket.

ADDRESS
The Green, Lurgashall
GU28 9ET

PHONE
01428 707346

WEBSITE
bestofengland.com/045

The Fox Goes Free

PUBLIC HOUSE | CHICHESTER | PO18 0HU

The Fox Goes Free is an alluring country pub in the quaint village of Charlton, West Sussex. The pub is 400 years old & full of oak beams, flint walls and open fireplaces. In warmer days, a pleasant afternoon can be spent in their large country garden overlooking the South Downs and nearby Goodwood Estate.

This listed building is surrounded by stunning, countryside walks. Wherever possible, their cuisine is locally sourced, home-made and includes favourites such as calamari and chorizo, fish pie and rib eye steak.

ADDRESS

Charlton Rd, Chichester
PO18 0HU

PHONE

01243 811461

WEBSITE

bestofengland.com/073

The Urchin

PUBLIC HOUSE | HOVE | BN3 3YS

The Urchin offers freshly caught shellfish from the Brighton coastline, as well as a wide selection of specialist craft beers. There are over 100 different types of beer to choose from and Brighton Gin is distilled in their cellar.

Located on a residential street in Hove, this pub is a true modern gem. Having opened in February 2015, The Urchin has already become a local institution and a destination.

263

ADDRESS

15-17 Belfast St, Hove
BN3 3YS

PHONE

01273 241881

WEBSITE

bestofengland.com/106

The White Hart

PUBLIC HOUSE | NETHERFIELD | TN33 9QH

The White Hart in Netherfield provides quality pub food in a relaxing environment. The pub is a family run free-house and restaurant run by Ron and Mel Birchall and offers a modern, locally sourced menu.

Farrow and Ball graces the walls and, when combined with an open fire, create an intimate and unpretentious atmosphere. The views from the terrace are also a spectacular place to have lunch or simply enjoy the vista.

ADDRESS

Darwell Hill, Battle
TN33 9QH

PHONE

01424 838382

WEBSITE

bestofengland.com/107

Duke of Cumberland

PUBLIC HOUSE | **FERNHURST** | GU27 3HQ

Nestling on the side of a steep hill in Henley near Fernhurst, is the picturesque Duke of Cumberland Arms. It dates back to the 16th century and benefits from breath-taking views and a delightful garden with ponds. Inside savour the old flagstones, rustic décor and local ales served straight from the barrel.

Roaring fireplaces in every room create a warm and unbeatable atmosphere throughout the winter, while in the summer sitting in the evening sun enjoying views across the Sussex and Surrey countryside is magical. An exciting menu uses local produce; including vegetables from the pubs own allotment.

ADDRESS
Henley nr Fernhurst
GU27 3HQ

PHONE
01428 652280

WEBSITE
bestofengland.com/040

The Horse Guards Inn

PUBLIC HOUSE | TILLINGTON | GU28 9AF

The Horse Guards Inn is located in the sleepy village of Tillington in the South Downs National Park, a few miles from Petworth. Filled with character, this 350-year-old pub is a great place to visit all year round. The vast, hidden garden is a picturesque haven of wild flowers and a great spot to catch the sun.

The interior is relaxed and inviting with plenty of seating, oak beams and open log fires. Their food uses the very best in local produce with the menu changing daily and with the seasons. There are three en-suite "country-chic" bedrooms.

ADDRESS
Upperton Rd, Tillington
GU28 9AF

PHONE
01798 342332

WEBSITE
bestofengland.com/085

28

29

The Lickfold Inn

PUBLIC HOUSE | PETWORTH | GU28 9EY

The Lickfold Inn near Petworth specialises in exceptional food, from bar snacks to contemporary fine dining. There is a busy restaurant on the first floor, and a more traditional pub atmosphere on the ground floor plus a large garden out back.

The pub is located on a quiet country road and is a great place to stop if you're walking in the splendid surroundings. The new chef Graham Squire has already received many accolades for the quality of his food; The pub has also recently been awarded "Best New Pub" in the Good Food Guide 2016.

ADDRESS

Highstead Lane, Lickfold,
Petworth
GU28 9EY

PHONE

01789 532535

WEBSITE

bestofengland.com/090

The Griffin

PUBLIC HOUSE | FLETCHING | TN22 3SS

Situated in the historic village of Fletching, The Griffin has been run by the Pullan family since 1979. During that time, The Griffin has built a considerable reputation for its food and wine. People come from far and wide to sample their cuisine.

The Griffin has a large, expertly landscaped garden with a stunning view over Sheffield Park. It includes a terrace area for al fresco dining, a large barbecue area and sloping lawns. 13 en suite bedrooms are available as featured in The Good Hotel Guide and Alistair Sawday's.

ADDRESS

High Street, Fletching
TN22 3SS

PHONE

01825 722890

WEBSITE

bestofengland.com/317

The Globe Inn Marsh

RYE | TN31 7NX | 01797 225220

A stones throw from the coast and a short stroll from Rye's town centre is the eclectic Globe Inn Marsh. A fantastic mish-mash of cosy fireplaces, unusual objects and stylish furnishings. As you walk through the door you'll see a fine selection of nibbles and artisan breads ready for dipping in stews and soups.

 bestofengland.com/303

31

Ancient Mariner

HOVE | BN3 5FE | 01273 748595

Hove has always been proud of its friendly, well-managed pubs and The Ancient Mariner definitely ticks a lot of boxes for those who love a relaxed pint of well-kept ale. This is a lovely local pub, hidden away from the hustle and bustle of Brighton, and enjoyed by locals as a top spot for a beer and a bite.

 bestofengland.com/037

262

Blackboys Inn

UCKFIELD | TN22 5LG | 01825 890283

On the outskirts of Uckfield, Blackboys Inn is a stunning 14th Century public house with large gardens. In summer it's a great place to sip your favourite tipple, while watching the pub ducks chase each other around the pretty gardens. Blackboys also has large fireplaces - perfect on those colder nights.

 bestofengland.com/039

32

Halfway Bridge

LODSWORTH | GU28 9BP | 01798 861281

The Halfway Bridge is a charming 17th century coaching inn in the lovely village of Lodsworth. It's brimming with character from the period beams and open fires, to the beer stools crafted from old whiskey barrels. You'll find light snacks and over 50 carefully selected wines and champagnes to choose from.

 bestofengland.com/041

33

Hobgoblin

BRIGHTON | BN1 4GU | 01273 682933

The Hobgoblin, also known as The Troll's Pantry in Brighton, is a lively pub specialising in beer and organic burgers. The pub's exterior walls are covered with striking street art and inside alternative music is a vital part of its DNA. We like the sound of the Escape Room and the gourmet dough balls.

 bestofengland.com/042

35

The Crown Inn

HORSHAM | RH13 8NH | 01403 710902

In the small country hamlet of Dial Post sits The Crown Inn. This charming pub is a welcome resting stop for travellers and locals to the area, boasting a warm rustic atmosphere and great food. Head chef James has built an impressive reputation for sophisticated locally sourced dishes.

 bestofengland.com/043

34

Lion and Lobster

BRIGHTON | BN1 2PS | 01273 327299

The Lion & Lobster is one of the oldest and best-loved pubs in Brighton. You'll relish the atmosphere here, from the cheerful bright pink exterior to the eclectic style inside. Set in a quiet street, not far from the seafront, this pub spans three floors with a hidden terrace and regency restaurant.

 bestofengland.com/044

261

Palmeira Pub

HOVE | BN3 3ES | 01273 720641

The Palmeira is a fantastic modern pub close to Palmeira Square, famed for its Regency architecture. The Palmeira provides a great local meeting spot for the surrounding area, full of friendly people of all ages. The large, open layout creates a spacious environment, perfect for a big gathering or quiet pint.

 bestofengland.com/046

260

Salehurst Halt

ROBERTSBRIDGE | TN32 5PH | 01580 880620

The Salehurst Halt is a delightful pub tucked alongside the church in Robertsbridge. It's the kind of place that epitomises all that a country pub should be, offering a relaxed environment within the surroundings of East Sussex. The idyllic setting affords great views over the Rother Valley.

 bestofengland.com/047

36

The Shepherd and Dog

FULKING | BN5 9LU | 01273 857382

A charismatic pub in a tranquil location. The Shepherd and Dog is a haven of real ale and hearty food. Dating back to the 18th century, this local has built a loyal following who love to come and enjoy the relaxed environment.

 bestofengland.com/048

37

The Anchor Bleu

BOSHAM | PO18 8LS | 01243 573956

The Anchor Bleu in Bosham is located on the water's edge with glorious views overlooking the boats and harbour. The locally sourced menu features a mix of pub classics and seasonal specials with three cosy rooms to dine in and a waterside terrace to enjoy when the weather is fine.

 bestofengland.com/049

38

The Angel Inn

PETWORTH | GU28 0BG | 01798 344445

The Angel Inn is a superb local pub close to Golden Square in the historic market town of Petworth. This lovely little pub has been serving locals and visitors since medieval times. Look out for the bar featuring ships beams, wooden floors and stone walls. There are six bedrooms for those who want to stay.

 bestofengland.com/050

39

The Bell Inn

TICEHURST | TN5 7AS | 01580 200300

The Bell Inn is located in the heart of Ticehurst and has recently benefited from an extensive refurbishment, transforming it into a large, impressive and distinctive public house. As well as a bar and restaurant, the pub has eleven high spec rooms to stay in.

 bestofengland.com/052

 40

The Better Half

HOVE | BN3 2RG | 01273 737869

The Better Half in Hove is one of the oldest public houses in the area and has recently benefited from an extensive refurbishment. the pub now celebrates 'the heart and soul' of British pub culture, providing a relaxed and welcoming environment for casual drinking and fine dining.

 bestofengland.com/54

259

The Black Horse

PETWORTH | GU28 0HL | 01798 342424

The Black Horse is a 16th Century Inn situated in the Sussex countryside near the popular village of Petworth. With extensive gardens and a cozy interior, you are greeted by roaring log fires and traditional ambience. The meu focuses on local produce and fresh fish due to its access to the South Coast.

 bestofengland.com/055

41

The Blacksmiths

CHICHESTER | PO20 7PR | 01243 785578

The Blacksmiths is an award-winning pub in Donnington near Chichester. With its cosy wood fires, extensive garden and fine cuisine, a passion for local food is at the heart of every plate. The kitchen team also use high quality ingredients from their own garden and farm.

 bestofengland.com/056

42

The Bolney Stage

BOLNEY | RH17 5RL | 01444 881200

The Bolney Stage in the pretty village of Bolney, near Haywards Heath oozes character with huge inglenook fireplaces, ancient flagstones and crooked beams aplenty. Hearty pub classics such as braised shoulder of lamb sit alongside more modern dishes like 'Sesame pressed spiced duck'.

 bestofengland.com/057

43

The Bricklayers Arms

MIDHURST | GU29 9BX | 01730 812084

The Bricklayers Arms in Midhurst is a warm and welcoming pub situated within a historic, Grade II listed building from the 17th century. This rustic pub is an honest, friendly drinking establishment, which benefits from an open fire and a friendly landlord.

 bestofengland.com/058

 44

The Bridge Inn

AMBERLEY | BN18 9LR | 01798 831619

The Bridge Inn, Amberley is a traditional country pub and kitchen, located in the heart of the South Downs National Park. This cosy, inviting Inn offers classic pub dishes, daily specials and real ales in a warm and welcoming atmosphere.

 bestofengland.com/059

45

The Bull Inn

DITCHLING | BN6 8TA | 01273 843147

The Bull in Ditchling is one of the oldest buildings in Ditchling village and has been welcoming travellers and locals for over 500 years. Located inside the South Downs National Park, yet the Bull is only 15 minutes from Brighton and the sea.

 bestofengland.com/060

46

The Cat Inn

W. HOATHLY | RH19 4PP | 01342 810369

The Cat Inn, West Hoathly, is a 16th century free house with four bedrooms. The village is a haven for walkers, ideally placed on the Western edge of the Ashdown Forest and the surrounding area is blessed with a plethora of attractive places to visit.

i bestofengland.com/061

47

The Chimney House

BRIGHTON | BN1 5DF | 01273 556708

The Chimney House is a traditional pub in the heart of Brighton next to the Seven Dials. Ingredients are sourced from within Sussex with fish from Shoreham and Newhaven, fruit and vegetables from local farms and glasshouses and meat from Garlic Wood Farm.

i bestofengland.com/062

258

The Coach and Horses

DANEHILL | RH17 7JF | 01825 740369

If you are one for good food in a traditional country setting then the Coach and Horses in Danehill is sure to fulfill your expectations. Situated on the edge of the Ashdown Forest and hidden down a country lane, the location is peaceful and rural and from a large garden you'll enjoy views of the Sussex Downs.

i bestofengland.com/063

48

The Crab and Lobster

SIDLESHAM | PO20 7NB | 01243 641233

The Crab and Lobster in Sidlesham, close to Pagham harbour, is a great spot for a short break by the sea. This restaurant with rooms is famous for its locally sourced food including fresh fish straight off the boat at Selsey and of course plenty of crabs and lobsters.

i bestofengland.com/064

49

The Cricketers Arms

BILLINGSHURST | RH14 0DG | 01403 700369

The Cricketers Arms is set in the splendid village of Wisborough Green, with lovely views overlooking the local village green. The chef has built up a reputation over the last 10 years for classic, good quality, home cooked grub, particularly for his themed food nights on the last Friday of each month.

i   bestofengland.com/065

50

The Crown

HASTINGS | TN34 3BN | 01424 465100

The Crown is an independent pub in Hastings old town between East Hill country park and the beach. It offers a welcoming environment with friendly staff and plenty of local regulars. They serve Hastings brewed real ale and a delicious selection of home cooked meals.

i   bestofengland.com/067

51

The Crown and Anchor

CHICHESTER | PO20 7EE | 01243 781712

The Crown and Anchor at Dell Quay is a waterside, 16th century pub situated at the head of the Fishbourne Channel within Chichester Harbour. The large bay windows and open terrace offer great views of the water and the perfect place to watch local sailors and sunsets throughout the year.

i   bestofengland.com/68

52

The Dean

CHICHESTER | PO18 0QX | 01243 811465

The Dean Ale & Cider house in Chichester is a pub with a warm and welcoming atmosphere. Popular with beer enthusiasts who enjoy the extensive range of well kept real ales plus a great selection of craft beers from around the world. Craft ciders are also a fixture, on hand pump and by the bottle.

i   bestofengland.com/069

53

The Earl Of March

CHICHESTER | PO18 0BQ | 01243 533993

The Earl of March is a delightful gastropub located in the village of Lavant, near Chichester in West Sussex. Giles Thompson, the former Executive Head Chef at the Ritz Hotel London, took over the pub in 2007. The pub dates back to the early 18th century and the decor is modern yet rustic.

 bestofengland.com/070

54

The Farm Tavern

BRIGHTON | BN3 1FB | 01273 779886

The Farm Tavern is an intimate, friendly, quirky and recently refurbished pub in Hove. This Cask Marque accredited pub prides itself on sourcing the highest quality local produce – from its gin, artisan bread to cheese and charcuterie.

 bestofengland.com/071

257

The Lamb Inn

WARTLING | BN27 1RY | 01323 832116

The Lamb Inn in Wartling, between Eastbourne and Bexhill, is a traditional country pub with bedrooms. Low beams and plenty of old fireplaces give the pub some great character. On tap they have a good selection of local beers and the menu is full of top quality, local ingredients.

 bestofengland.com/072

55

The Fox Inn

HORSHAM | RH12 3JP | 01403 822386

The Fox Inn dates back to the early 16th century. The pub offers traditional pub food as well as Chinese dishes such as peanut and coconut curry and sweet and sour pork ribs. The wealth of original features including inglenook fireplaces and oak beams create a warm and enticing environment.

 bestofengland.com/074

56

The George and the Dragon

HORSHAM | RH13 8GE | 01403 741320

The George and Dragon is a small pub located in the idyllic village of Shipley. The pub prides itself on their selection of real ales. Dishes include roast guinea fowl, ham hock and their popular "Dragon Burger". There is a large garden with a childrens' play area to keep the little ones entertained.

 bestofengland.com/075

57

The George Inn

ROBERTSBRIDGE | TN32 5AW | 01580 880315

The George Inn is an 18th century coaching Inn situated in the charming village of Robertsbridge. They pride themselves on local produce and have an award winning restaurant serving local ales and wines from the region.

 bestofengland.com/076

58

The Corner House

WORTHING | BN11 1DJ | 01903 413852

The Corner House is a stylish and welcoming pub owned by brothers Tim and Matt Taylor. Cosy and vintage, the Corner House is the ideal place to relax with family and friends. Dishes are classics such as smoked salmon sandwiches, house burgers and classic fish & chips.

 bestofengland.com/077

59

The George Payne

HOVE | BN3 5HB | 01273 329563

The George Payne in Hove was refurbished in 2012, when its new owners Zoe and Steve gave it a complete transformation, winning an award for 'Best Turnaround Pub in Britain' along the way. Since then, the pub has become a key meeting place for many local groups and a great community resource.

 bestofengland.com/078

253

The Green Man

HORSHAM | RH13 8JT | 01403 710250

The Green Man is run by husband and wife team Becky and Nick Illes. Chef Nick has a background working in some of London's top hotel restaurants and has brought his little black book of specialist suppliers and his passion for sourcing the finest ingredients to the pub.

 bestofengland.com/080

60

The Hare and Hounds

BRIGHTON | BN1 4JF | 01273 682839

The Hare & Hounds, on London Road, has benefitted from an extensive and stylish recent refurbishment. The pub offers a wide selection of craft beers and local ales, while on the food front, they have teamed up with local institution, La Choza, to offer an interesting menu of Mexican street food.

 bestofengland.com/084

254

The Inglenook

B. REGIS | PO21 3QB | 01243 262495

The Inglenook is a 16th century Hotel & Restaurant in Bognor Regis, with lots different areas to explore and enjoy. From bars with low beams and fireplaces, to a garden room, restaurant and large pub garden, The Inglenook has it all.

 bestofengland.com/086

61

The Kings Arms

FERNHURST | GU27 3HA | 01428 641165

The Kings Arms in Fernhurst is on the road between Midhurst and Haslemere in the gorgeous South Downs. Inside this Grade II listed building, there's a restaurant and bar as well as six luxurious ensuite bedrooms which are located within a converted stable block.

 bestofengland.com/087

62

The Lamb Inn

WITTERING | PO20 8QA | 01243 511105

The Lamb Inn in West Wittering is a great place to stop for a bite to eat and a drink, after visiting the surrounding countryside. The Lamb is rightly proud of the reputation they have for offering fantastic food, ranging from light lunches through to dinners and epic Sunday lunches.

 bestofengland.com/088

 63

The George at Burpham

BURPHAM | BN18 9RR | 01903 883131

By the locals, for the locals, of the locals - and a very warm welcome to everyone'. The George at Burpham is an award winning village pub that seeks to provide excellent food in a friendly setting. This traditional 17th century pub is a particular favourite among dog walkers and hikers.

 bestofengland.com/089

 64

The Lion

PAGHAM | PO21 3JX | 01243 262149

The Lion Inn, Bognor Regis was once a popular smugglers' haunt, which dates back to the 14th century. Now its old oak beams and open fireplaces offer a welcoming atmosphere where you can enjoy the choice of fine dining or bar specials.

 bestofengland.com/092

 65

The Mermaid Inn

RYE | TN31 7EY | 01797 223065

The Mermaid Inn is situated in the beautiful town of Rye, on a fantastic cobbled street full of history. The Inn has maintained the essence of true English charm for over 800 years and still has original features including a cellar dating back to 1156.

 bestofengland.com/093

66

The North Laine

BRIGHTON | BN1 4AA | 01273 683666

The North Laine Pub in Brighton is the home of the Laine Brewing microbrewery, and a great place to join brewers and fans of craft beers enjoying a wide range of different styles of ales and lagers. The spacious layout is full of character, creating a relaxed environment to enjoy your favourite tipple.

 bestofengland.com/094

256

The Playden Oasts

RYE | TN31 7UL | 01797 22 502

The Playden Oasts Inn is nestled in the lovely village of Playden near Rye on the Kent and East Sussex border and many of the original features of the oast building can be found in this unique public house.

 bestofengland.com/095

67

The Queens Head

SEDLESCOMBE | TN33 0QA | 01424 870228

The Queens Head is a 14th century, family run pub situated in the heart of the beautiful and idyllic village of Sedlescombe. Low beams and a large fireplace create a homely atmosphere throughout, while the back room showcases some great local art.

 bestofengland.com/097

68

The Rose Cottage

ALCISTON | BN26 6UW | 01323 870377

The Rose Cottage Inn is a traditional pub located in Alciston, in the heart of the South Downs National Park. Owned by the same family for over 40 years, the pub is surrounded by stunning countryside scenery, a wide selection of walks and, at weekends, you may stumble across a Morris Dancer or two.

 bestofengland.com/099

69

The Royal Oak

WHATLINGTON | TN33 0NJ | 01424 870492

The Royal Oak in Whatlington, dates back to the 15th century. With a wealth of original features including the large inglenook fireplace, the 80ft indoor well, quirky olde-world interior and private large beer garden, The Royal Oak is the perfect place to meet up with friends and family.

 bestofengland.com/100

70

The Stag Inn

PETWORTH | GU28 9JP | 01403 820241

The Stag Inn is an enticing and renowned country pub set within the charming village of Balls Cross near Petworth. Log fires welcome you while the candlelit restaurant invites you to sample the culinary delights including dishes like pheasant breast, lambs liver and garlic calamari.

 bestofengland.com/101

71

The Standard Inn

RYE | TN31 7EN | 01797 225231

The Standard Inn, Rye is situated in the heart of the citadel. The pub has been recently restored to its 15th century glory, with beautifully carved beams and open fires. The menu is fish led with dishes such as 'Rye bay king scallops, five spice pork belly and celeriac puree'.

 bestofengland.com/102

72

The Star Inn

WALDRON | TN21 0RA | 01435 812495

The Star Inn is a friendly pub with bags of character. Heavy beams, knotty wood floors and great open fireplaces, add to the atmosphere. Set in the quiet village of Waldron, this pub offers a great choice of food and a fine selection of real ales, beers and cider.

 bestofengland.com/103

73

The Three Crowns

BILLINGSHURST | RH14 0DX | 01403 700239

The Three Crowns in Wisborough Green is a quaint village Pub, with great food. The owners make the effort to source their ingredients from local farms, butchers and bakers and seek out a variety of local ales. Due to its great reputation the Pub can get very busy, so it's best to book in advance for food.

 bestofengland.com/104

74

The Tiger Inn

E. DEAN | BN20 0DA | 01323 423209

Set in the heart of picturesque East Dean, the Tiger Inn is a great 16th century pub to stop off at after a walk along the Seven Sisters. The Tiger Inn offers local real ales including Beachy Head which is brewed within walking distance of the pub.

 bestofengland.com/105

75

The White Horse

PULBOROUGH | RH20 2DY | 01798 872189

The White Horse in Pulborough is a country inn, with history dating back to 1866. The interior decor is simple but cosy, creating an enticing environment in which to sit back and enjoy a pint or two.

 bestofengland.com/108

76

The White Lion

THAKEHAM | RH20 3EP | 01798 813141

The White Lion in Thakeham is an original old coaching inn situated in the heart of this picturesque West Sussex village. The pub has kept many of its traditional features and added new elements of character over the years.

 bestofengland.com/109

77

The White Swan

BOSHAM | PO18 8NG | 01243 696465

The White Swan in Bosham is a lovely little pub dating back to the 18th Century. The grade II listed free house provides a selection of ales and seasonal dishes throughout the year and is definitely worth a visit if you're in the area.

 bestofengland.com/110

78

The Windmill Inn

HORSHAM | RH13 8EJ | 01403 710308

The Windmill Inn of Littleworth first opened its doors in 1909 and is named after Jolesfield Windmill, an eight-sided tarred smock mill that stood in the village until the early 1960s. This charming pub has recently been renovated and is located 20 minutes south of Horsham or 20 minutes north of Worthing.

 bestofengland.com/111

79

Ypres Castle Inn

RYE | TN31 7HH | 01797 223248

The Ypres Castle Inn in Rye, is reached via the 1697 Gun Garden steps and has been serving locals since the 1600's. Dishes include Rye Bay Scallops, Rye Bay Plaice, local crab and John Dory on the seasonal menu. There is a large pub garden with views across Romney Marsh where you can watch the sunset.

 bestofengland.com/112

80

The Rising Sun

NUTBOURNE | RH20 2HE | 01798 812191

The Rising Sun in Nutbourne is a delightful village pub close to Pulborough. The comfortable bar area has a great selection of local beers and ales and is an ideal space for events, live music or just putting your feet up by the fire.

 bestofengland.com/300

81

The Gardeners Arms

WAKEHURST | RH17 6TJ | 01444 892328

Some of Sussex's finest gardens and days out are to be enjoyed near to The Gardeners Arms. Their seasonal menu, offers a range of fresh produce from pub favourites such as shepherd's pie to smoked haddock chowder. On tap is the great range of ales and there is also a decent sized garden.

 bestofengland.com/113

82

The Kings Arms

ROTHERFIELD | TN6 3LJ | 01892 853441

The Kings Arms has a fine country-pub feel and is located in the quaint village of Rotherfield. Fires roar throughout the colder months warming walkers, and in the summer, the huge garden is perfect for Al Fresco dining with views over the Ashdown Forest.

 bestofengland.com/114

83

The Ship

RYE | TN31 7DB | 01797 222233

The Ship Inn is situated in the centre of Rye, at the bottom of the infamous Mermaid Street. Built in 1592 and originally used as a warehouse for storing contraband seized from smugglers. The menu focuses on local, sustainable and organic ingredients and stays closely connected to the seasons.

 bestofengland.com/306

84

The Lewes Arms

LEWES | BN7 1YH | 01273 473152

The Lewes Arms in Mount Place is a pub with barrels of character and an idiosyncratic bunch of customers to match. Pea throwing, poetry and pantomime along with dwyle flunking (no, me neither) are just some of the pursuits you may find going on if you pop in for a pint.

 bestofengland.com/318

251

PDF Downloads

All of our travel guides are available to buy as downloadable PDFs.

You can keep them on your Desktop, Phone or Tablet and browse all of our lovely photography in high resolution.

Visit our shop bestofengland.shop to find out more.

BEST OF ENGLAND
INSPIRING DISCOVERY

CHAPTER THREE
Cafés & Tea Rooms

Beehive on The Green

CAFÉ | EAST DEAN | BN20 0BY

The Beehive on The Green is a small, independent delicatessen and café located in the pretty village of East Dean. The café serves classic light bites and the large windows and tables outside offer views over the picturesque green and beyond to the South Downs.

The inside is very comfortable, with attractive furnishings and a great selection of good produce. The Deli has a wide range of cheeses and meats and the shop sells award-winning local breads and beers. The Beehive on the Green is in a lovely location with dramatic coast around the corner.

ADDRESS

The Green, East Dean
BN20 0BY

PHONE

01323 423631

WEBSITE

bestofengland.com/119

Amberley Tearoom

CAFÉ | AMBERLEY | BN18 9SR

This quaint Tearoom in Amberley is full of rural charm and character. Renowned for their cream teas and home-baked scones with traditional clotted cream, their indulgent cakes are generous and their menu includes Gluten Free options. Friendly staff help to create a warm and relaxing ambience.

The wood-burner, original wooden beams and high-ceilings within this Grade II listed building reinforce an olde world charm. The coffee is roasted locally and the crockery is from the pottery in Amberley. The Tearoom is open from March and closed in winter.

ADDRESS

The Square Amberley, Arundel
BN18 9SR

PHONE

01798 839196

WEBSITE

bestofengland.com/118

87

The Singing Kettle

CAFÉ | ALFRISTON | BN26 5UD

The Singing Kettle is a small homely café in the heart of Alfriston. With a fine selection of cakes and light lunches. This bright and friendly café is a great afternoon stop off, when exploring the village.

The large window at the front gives you fantastic views onto Alfriston market, to be enjoyed while indulging in the tearoom's renowned cream-teas.

ADDRESS
6 Waterloo Square, Alfriston,
Polegate
BN26 5UD

PHONE
01323 870723

WEBSITE
bestofengland.com/115

88

Café Elvira

CAFÉ | HAYWARDS HEATH | RH16 1XP

Café Elvira is located within the Borde Hill Gardens a few miles north of Haywards Heath. The café is an attractive space and makes a great option for lunch when visiting the gardens. They have a delicious selection of homemade cakes, a light lunch menu from the blackboard and very tasty afternoon teas.

They have a large seating area outside, so you can continue your garden experience and fresh flowers on every table light up the café and make it more homely. Café Elvira is also licensed and offers a good choice of spirits and wines, many of which are from the local area.

ADDRESS

Borde Hill, Borde Hill Gardens
RH16 1XP

PHONE

01444 458845

WEBSITE

bestofengland.com/116

Mama Ghanoushe

CAFÉ | HASSOCKS | BN6 8AH

Mama Ghanoushe is a bright and vibrant café situated on the high street of Hassocks. It brings us something new and exciting, only selling vegetarian and raw sugar free vegan treats, all of which are gluten free and suitable for people with coeliac disease.

The owner Rachel, has had many years experience working as a Cordon Bleu trained chef and now puts her expertise into this little café which serves excellent food. The bright colours and fresh, open feel create a calm and comfortable environment in which you can relax and unwind with a little treat.

ADDRESS
31 Keymer Rd, Hassocks
BN6 8AH

PHONE
01273 842534

WEBSITE
bestofengland.com/117

91

The Courtyard

CAFÉ | ROTHERFIELD | TN6 3LL

The Courtyard Cafe in Rotherfield feels cosy and very civilised, an open spaced room with a good cake selection on the counter. Gifts, sweets and crafts are available for purchase towards the back and as the name suggests, they have a courtyard where you can eat in the sun.

During the cooler months you'll have to fight for the tables by the pot belly stove where you can warm your toes and tuck into a tasty bowl of soup. They also have regular supper clubs where you can enjoy some worldly flavours.

ADDRESS

6A High Street, Rotherfield,
Crowborough
TN6 3LL

PHONE

01892 852333

WEBSITE

bestofengland.com/120

Fig

CAFÉ | RYE | TN31 7JE

The Fig in Rye is a new stylish coffee house and bistro with a short menu focusing on healthy, wholesome dishes with exciting vegetarian options. You can expect a fine breakfast and for lunch they offer salads, soups and daily specials. The layout is clean and simple yet warm and inviting.

On the grind is renowned for Monmouth Coffee from London, roasted and delivered within a day, it's fresh as spring and tastes delightful.

92

ADDRESS
2 High St, Rye
TN31 7JE

PHONE
01797 690643

WEBSITE
bestofengland.com/304

Barley Sugar

CAFÉ | EASTBOURNE | BN21 4NN

Barley Sugar is a top-class independent Delicatessen and Cafe delivering the goods to the public of Eastbourne and beyond. They specialise in high quality produce and their deli offers a unique choice of artisan breads, cheeses, cured and cooked meats, chocolates, cakes and more.

Their cafe offers something a little better than your average panini lunch and uses a collection of fine ingredients from the deli next-door. Tempations include; chicken, courgette and cracked pepper popletti and grilled pear tartine. They also have a decent selection of vintage goodies in their lifestyle store.

ADDRESS

1 Cornfield Terrace, Eastbourne
BN21 4NN

PHONE

01323 729577

WEBSITE

bestofengland.com/305

Nelson Coffee Co

CAFÉ | EASTBOURNE | BN21 3LP

Nelson Coffee Co in Eastbourne has certainly mastered the art of a great coffee, their other hot drinks are pretty special too with mega hot chocolates and speciality tea. Being as good as it is and being located beside the train station makes for a popular spot, but don't let that stop you.

The staff are super friendly and this level of finesse and is hard to come by in Eastbourne. They also have plenty of bites to choose from including homemade sausage rolls and bad-boy pastrami sandwiches. If you're into coffee and are in the area then Nelson Coffee Co should be high on your list.

ADDRESS

4 Terminus Rd, Eastbourne
BN21 3LP

PHONE

01323 301150

WEBSITE

bestofengland.com/307

94

Mr T's

CAFÉ | FLETCHING | TN22 3SS

Mr T's is Fletching's Village Shop. Run by the ever friendly Jason, this shop come deli provides a valuable village service as well as a popular destination for cyclists to stop off for a coffee and a cake before their return leg back home.

Lattes, cappuccinos and teas are available as well as a wide range of sandwiches, meats, milk and cheese. Everything you need from a local village store. They're child friendly and even have a box of toys ready to keep the little ones entertained. On a sunny day you can sit outside and watch the world go by.

ADDRESS

High Street, Fletching
TN22 3SS

PHONE

01825 723175

WEBSITE

bestofengland.com/309

Billycan Coffee

CAFÉ | HASTINGS | TN34 1JU

Dubbed 'the best coffee in Hastings', Billycan Coffee is a little coffee kiosk located on Hastings pier, serving Union Hand Roasted artisan coffee, plus smoothies and sweet delights. The owners have a passion for creating the finest quality, high-end products served in the most welcoming of atmospheres.

The two owners met through performing at the circus but wanted to escape to build a life together by the sea. After helping to rebuild Hastings pier, they were given the opportunity to open Billycan. The coffee kiosk is now thriving and popular and people come from far and wide to experience their coffee.

ADDRESS

1-10 White Rock, Hastings
TN34 1JU

PHONE

N/A

WEBSITE

bestofengland.com/121

Hector's Shed

CAFÉ | SHOREHAM | BN43 5ZD

Hector's Shed is a quirky little café & shop located in Shoreham-by-Sea, on a popular street corner. This is a lovely local café, serving all kinds of great quality cakes and snacks, along with a huge selection of hot and cold drinks.

Inside you'll find all sorts of interesting and quirky items dotted around the shop. The décor takes on a cool rustic look, similar to a farm shop. There is a small outside seating area, as well as more tables inside, with big windows to sit beside and watch the world go by.

ADDRESS

36 East St, Shoreham-by-Sea
BN43 5ZD

PHONE

01273 463950

 97

bestofengland.com/163

Saltmarsh Kitchen

CAFÉ | SEAFORD | BN25 4AD

Whether you're out walking or pausing before heading to the beach, the charming 16th century farmhouse of Saltmarsh is the best place around Cuckmere Haven and the Seven Sisters Country Park for decent grub.

With a spacious walled garden, plenty of seating, three bright tastefully decorated rooms, huge fireplaces and locally sourced quality food; saltmarsh is well worth a visit. If you intend to stay in this beautiful location, Saltmarsh also have six beautifully finished guestrooms in their private house.

ADDRESS

Exceat, Cuckmere
Valley, Seaford
BN25 4AD

PHONE

01323 870218

 98

bestofengland.com/122

Mozzino

CAFÉ | BRIGHTON | BN2 3HQ

Expect a warm welcome when entering Coffee Bar, Mozzino. This café is the second of its kind after the first was such a hit in Soho, London. The founder began collecting vintage coffee machines from the 1950s and naturally, fell in love with all things bean related.

This café has a vast, inviting counter. Stacked high with parma-ham sandwiches, mozzarella and other delectable treats. The walls are studded with Italian collectibles and there is a Capri-esq patio to the back. The coffee is excellent; you can almost taste the passion behind it.

ADDRESS

38 Lewes Rd, Brighton
BN2 3HQ

PHONE

N/A

248

bestofengland.com/123

The Flour Pot

CAFÉ | BRIGHTON | BN1 4EP

The Flour Pot Bakery is in the heart of the famous Laines in Brighton and is the result of founder Oli Hyde's commitment to all things artisanal. It is the perfect place to grab yourself a tasty treat. Their wide selection of fresh bread is a must try.

After initial success as a bakery, The Flour Pot team have developed their café into a buzzing hub for locals where they serve up delicious fresh food for breakfast, brunch and lunch, with great coffee to match.

ADDRESS

40 Sydney St, Brighton
BN1 4EP

PHONE

01273 621942

249

bestofengland.com/124

Small Batch Coffee

CAFÉ | BRIGHTON | BN1 2AA

With the Brighton Pavilion as their company logo, Small Batch is a proud, Sussex company serving delicious coffee to customers throughout Brighton and Hove. They now have a number of stores and this, the latest, is located in Western Road.

The decor is sleek and simplistic with plenty of space to sit down after a busy shopping day. Selecting the right coffee beans is no simple job. Small Batch takes into account the altitude, harvest and processing methods to ensure coffee is of the best quality.

ADDRESS

111 Western Rd,
Brighton
BN1 2AA

PHONE

01273 731077

250

bestofengland.com/125

Mrs Burton's

CAFÉ | BATTLE | TN33 0AE

Mrs Burton's Tea Rooms in Battle is situated almost opposite the world famous Battle Abbey. This makes it an ideal place to stop when visiting the town. The quaint interior of the building dates back to the 16th century, giving it a cosy ambiance and homely feel.

The tea room is open throughout the week and serves a great selection of traditional British food. When it's busy expect to be rubbing shoulders, as the space is relatively small, but that said it adds to the character. If it's warm there's a large seating area outside the front and back.

ADDRESS

2 High St, Battle
TN33 0AE

PHONE

01424 774204

99

bestofengland.com/126

Judges Bakery

CAFÉ | ROBERTSBRIDGE | TN32 5AL

Judges Bakery in Robertsbridge is a quaint cafe, offering some top notch produce. The wide selection of cakes will make your mouth water. As well as cakes they provide healthier, home baked produce and good quality coffee.

The village of Robertsbridge is very attractive and well worth a walk around. The old timber framed buildings and quaint streets are full of history. Judges is a great place to stop in between sightseeing.

ADDRESS

51 High St, Roberts-
bridge
TN32 5AL

PHONE

01580 880434

100

bestofengland.com/127

Flint Owl Bakery

CAFÉ | LEWES | BN7 2NS

Flint Owl is passionate about bread and their loaves, croissants and pastries are all handcrafted and baked in small batch sizes using ingredients that are organic and of only the highest quality. Regionally renowned for their artisanal craftsmanship, they supply some of the top restaurants, cafes and shops.

Flint Owl cafe is situated in the heart of Lewes and offers an artful array of loaves positioned next to sweet baked breakfast pastries and cakes. Vibrant bowls of healthy salads are available for take-away lunches and a pretty walled courtyard garden allows for al fresco lunching on warmer days.

ADDRESS

209 High Street, Lewes
BN7 2NS

PHONE

01273 472769

101

bestofengland.com/128

The Marwood

CAFÉ | BRIGHTON | BN1 1AF

Located in Brighton's Laines, Marwood Coffee is a café with a quirky edge. It is well known for its eccentric individual interior, as well as its tasty homemade cakes, and coffee. It is the perfect representation of Brighton, all squeezed into a little coffee shop.

They have recently opened a kitchen, which they describe as 'no ordinary kitchen'. Cooking up deliciously different meals. With its secret garden you can enjoy the sunshine outside or sit inside and enjoy the café's unusual aesthetic.

ADDRESS

52 Ship Street,
Brighton
BN1 1AF

PHONE

01273 382063

 147

bestofengland.com/129

Tarrant Street Espresso

CAFÉ | ARUNDEL | BN18 9DG

Tarrant Street Espresso is an independent coffee shop on the popular high street of Arundel. This small, trendy café is the perfect place to take a break whilst in Arundel. While only being a small café, it still provides great quality coffee with a large selection of cakes and sandwiches.

The massive window covering the front of the store allows for lots of natural light and a great chance to people watch. It's great for a quick coffee to sit in or grab and go.

ADDRESS

17 Tarrant St, Arundel
BN18 9DG

PHONE

01903 885350

 102

bestofengland.com/130

"The designer's job is
to imagine the world
not how it is, but how
it should be."

T. Conran

Comestibles

MIDHURST | GU29 9PB | 01730 813400

Comestibles in Midhurst is a great Café and Deli tucked along the old, pretty, back streets of the town. With only a few tables, the café fills up fast and is generally busy with locals and visitors, but not to worry, there are a few more tables outside.

 bestofengland.com/131

103

Ginger & Dobbs

SHOREHAM | BN43 5ZD | 01273 453359

Ginger and Dobbs is a lovely little café and greengrocers located in Shorham-by-Sea. The store provides a relaxed homely atmosphere and a great place to enjoy a coffee and selection of home baked cakes. The greengrocers are stocked up daily with fruit and veg, local eggs and homemade bread and pastries.

 bestofengland.com/132

104

NRG Cavern

WORTHING | BN11 3BA | 01903 207777

Mark Reynolds and Alan Bentley opened NRG Cavern in Worthing in June 2015, with the vision to help and educate others on healthy eating. On their own individual journeys to change and improve their lifestyles, they found it really hard to find balanced nutritional food cooked when wanting to eat in or take out.

 bestofengland.com/133

105

The Toll House

LINDFIELD | RH16 2HL | 01444 482200

For a truly distinctive shopping and dining experience visit The Toll House Store & café in the heart of Lindfield. Billed as 'possibly the smallest department store in Sussex,' and housed in a former 17th-century tollgate, this much loved spot offers coffee, tea and cakes, breakfast and lunch options.

 bestofengland.com/134

106

Knoops

RYE | TN13 7LD | 01797 225838

Knoops is a modest Café in Rye, which has made a name for its luxurious hot chocolates, they are described as the 'purveyors of the finest hot chocolate'. The menu is dedicated solely to hot chocolate. They serve 3 strengths of cocoa (30, 50 and 70%) with a wide variety of flavourings (all fresh, no syrups).

 bestofengland.com/135

 107

Highdown Tea Rooms

WORTHING | BN12 6FB | 01903 246984

This lovely tearooms is hidden away on Highdown Hill, on the South Downs. It's very popular, so if you're lucky enough to get a table outside then it's perfect for a summer's day. The staff are very welcoming to customers on both two and four legs, making it the perfect stop off after a dog walk up the downs.

 bestofengland.com/136

 108

Fika

LINDFIELD | RH16 2HL | 01444 483027

Fika is a lovely traditional village tea room on Lindfield's high street. The shop is well decorated and benefits from excellent natural lighting. This creates a great atmosphere for you to enjoy something from their selection of quality teas and coffees, home-made cakes and fresh sandwiches.

 bestofengland.com/137

109

Café Plenty

BRIGHTON | BN1 4GW | 01273 387649

Café Plenty is a vibrant new enterprise in Brighton. It opened in Easter 2016, and has been a hive of buzzing activity ever since. Here you can expect to find a delicious selection of cakes and breads made in their micro-bakery. They also offer sandwiches, pies and salads.

 bestofengland.com/138

110

Le Magasin

LEWES | BN7 2AN | 01273 474720

Le Magasin is one of the best cafés in Lewes, and is new to the foodie scene on Cliffe High Street. The building is not only a café but a bistro and wine bar as well. Le Magasin is a fully licensed bistro, offering a range of European cuisines.

 bestofengland.com/139

246

Badger's Teahouse

ALFRISTON | BN26 5UG | 01323 871336

It's no wonder Badger's have gained such great press coverage, for their amazing tearooms based in Alfriston; with an attractive garden, stylish layout, mouth-watering cakes, classic crockery and friendly service. It certainly has the essence of an old fashioned tearoom.

 bestofengland.com/140

112

Pooh Corner

HARTFIELD | TN7 4AE | 01892 770456

The world famous Pooh Corner in Hartfield is home to the worlds largest selection of "Pooh Phernalia." Browse through thousands of souvenirs and visit Piglets Tearoom and Garden, where they serve tasty light lunches and specials such as Tigger's Treats, Smackerels, Strengthening Medicines and plenty more.

 bestofengland.com/141

113

Wilderness Woods Café

HAD. DOWN | TN22 4HJ | 01825 830509

Tucked away in the woods in Hadlow Down, with a forest school and shop, this alluring Café is the perfect place to relax in front of the fire with a book or look out over the rolling countryside. When it's warm you can sit out the back and watch the kids' eyes light up with all the hidden treasures dotted around the forest.

 bestofengland.com/142

114

Coffeetzar

BRIGHTON | BN1 4ER | 01273 628881

With its simplistic white exterior and shabby chic cake display, Coffeetzar is a treat for the eyes and the mouth. This independent coffee shop in Brighton is a bustling place to enjoy a French pastry and warming latte.

 bestofengland.com/143

115

The West Dean Stores

W. DEAN | PO18 0QY | 01243 818222

West Dean Stores and Tea Room is the sort of place every little village craves. They have a wide selection of local, fresh produce, newspapers and basic essentials. They also sell free range eggs, have daily deliveries of bread and freshly made sandwiches.

 bestofengland.com/144

116

The Boulevard

WITTERING | PO20 8DZ | 01243 672617

The Boulevard in East Wittering offers a wide range of food throughout the day. They offer plenty of classic dishes, and occasionally have specials such as Lobster and Sole when in season. The Boulevard is generally busy and has a lot of locals who visit regularly.

 bestofengland.com/145

117

The Mermaid Street Café

RYE | TN31 7EU | 01797 222128

The Mermaid Street Café is well situated on the corner of one of Rye's most picturesque streets. With a great seating area outside you can enjoy the historical charm, with a tasty fresh cake and hot drink. The Café has a simple yet delicious menu with homemade goodies.

 bestofengland.com/146

118

Pilgrims Rest

BATTLE | TN33 0AE | 01424 772314

The Pilgrims Rest is located inside a building which is over 800 years old, and is situated next to one of England's finest examples of English history, in the small town of Battle. The cakes are fantastic and the fireplace makes the café a warm and comfortable place to enjoy something special.

 bestofengland.com/148

119

I Gigi Café

BRIGHTON | BN3 1AF | 01273 728160

I Gigi general store in Hove is an inspiring womenswear and interiors boutique with a popular in-store Café. Stripped back wooden floors and whitewashed walls set the backdrop to its soft palette of grey velvet furnishings and rustic glass chandeliers.

 bestofengland.com/149

120

Orangery Tea Room

BATTLE | TN33 9NF | 01424 894203

The Orangery Tea Rooms at Ashburnham Place are well worth a visit. The large bright glasshouse is considered a conservatory and has wonderful views over the immaculate grounds. The high ceilings and plants in the Tea Room make it a joy to sit and relax over the finest produce.

 bestofengland.com/150

121

Coffee at 33

BRIGHTON | BN1 4ED | 01273 462460

Unlike many Cafés, Coffee at 33 brews its own coffee. This unique, understated Café in Brighton has been running for just a few years, and is a safe yet delicious bet for a Flat White. The blueberry, lemon and coconut slice is a must.

 bestofengland.com/151

252

CHAPTER FOUR
Places to Shop

Sparks Yard

SHOP | **ARUNDEL** | **BN18 9DJ**

Sparks Yard was opened in 2003 by Holly and Andy Heggadon, within a Grade II listed Victorian building in the heart of Arundel. They specialise in contemporary gifts, homeware and cookware. Popular from day one, the shop has since expanded over the three floors and now includes a restaurant on the top floor.

The shop is bright, colourful and stylish. Holly and Andy take their inspiration from California, both in terms of layout and the products they offer. Perfect if you need a bit of inspiration for those hard to find gifts.

ADDRESS

18 Tarrant St, Arundel
BN18 9DJ

PHONE

01903 885588

WEBSITE

bestofengland.com/153

Gun Room Shop

SHOP | ALFRISTON | BN26 5TL

This lovely quaint shop, referred to as The Gun Room, is the retail outlet for Rathfinny. The old, barn style building was said to have been the gun store for the Duke of Wellington in past time. It is situated on the Tye, the picturesque village common in Alfriston.

The outlet specialises in locally sourced and wine related products but also stocks other interesting gifts. Rathfinny's first still wine 'Cradle Valley' is now available to taste and purchase in the shop. The shop is also used as a place for visitors to book wine tours around their estate.

ADDRESS

The Tye, Alfriston, Polegate
BN26 5TL

PHONE

01323 870022

WEBSITE

bestofengland.com/152

Ivory & Pitch

SHOP | WESTBOURNE | PO10 8UJ

Ivory & Pitch has a wide choice of stylish homewares, carefully selected from across Europe, including glassware, china, linens and textiles, and vintage furniture. The store is a destination for original pieces, offering a mix of modern country and urban style.

Owner Caroline, is an expert in Chalk Paint™, trained by Annie Sloan, and runs monthly paint workshops for all levels, sharing her knowledge and passion for transforming furniture.

ADDRESS

6 The Grove, Westbourne
PO10 8UJ

PHONE

01243 377813

WEBSITE

bestofengland.com/154

Wittering Surf Shop

SHOP | WITTERING | PO20 8DY

The Drift-In Surf Café and the Surf Shop is one large building separated into several rooms. They have amazing clothing with great branding and everything you need to ride the waves with boards, shades and some fab wetsuits. Their Café has some of the best coffee in town in a rustic, comfortable setting.

You can tell when visiting that a lot of time and effort has been put into designing the space, the small details add to the character. As well as the Café and shop they also have a great selection of tasty ice-creams and their very own radio station.

125

Spencer Swaffer

SHOP | ARUNDEL | BN18 9AB

Spencer Swaffer Antiques is an achingly stylish, incredible treasure chest of intriguing objects and furniture that has been a feature of the High Street of Arundel for the past 20 years. There are several rooms to get lost within and a stunning floral garden to the rear.

Swaffer has been in the antiques business for over 35 years and has an extensive range of objects for sale. From very traditional to very quirky, there are four large floors of painted and decorative furniture, lighting, seating and accessories.

ADDRESS
30 High Street, Arundel
BN18 9AB

PHONE
01903 882132

WEBSITE
bestofengland.com/188

The Patchwork Dog & Basket

SHOP | LEWES | BN7 1YH

The Patchwork Dog and Basket is a little quilting and haberdashery shop, in the heart of Lewes. They specialise in patchwork and quilting, selling pretty much everything you'll need to make a quilt. Whether you're a beginner or a pro they'll have the stuff you need.

Bunting is draped from all corners of the ceiling creating a cave of pretty colours and fabrics. The shop also hosts a range of events for all ages as well as different courses and workshops.

ADDRESS
2 Mount Place, Lewes
BN7 1YH

PHONE
01273 483886

WEBSITE
bestofengland.com/157

127

Anthony Short Antiques

SHOP | PETWORTH | GU28 0AH

Anthony Short Antiques first opened a gallery 10 years ago in Antwerp, following his father's footsteps, who has been in the antiques trade for more than 40 years. In 2008 he moved to Petworth and started dealing in antiques from his shop on East Street.

The shop stocks a large collection of 17th, 18th and 19th century quality antique furniture, decorative antique objects, antique prints and also antique silver. At Anthony Short Antiques all products are genuine and bought specifically with a keen eye on contemporary trends to complement modern living.

ADDRESS
Market Square, Petworth
GU28 0AH

PHONE
01798 344092

WEBSITE
bestofengland.com/158

128

W.F. Bruce Antique Clocks

SHOP | LEWES | BN7 2PA

W.F.Bruce was established in 1985. Initially based on the outskirts of Lewes but larger premises were soon required and the business moved to the village of Herstmonceux, before returning to Lewes and settling on North street in 2002.

The shop has two large well-stocked showrooms and excellent workshop facilities, where sympathetic restoration of the stock is undertaken. Often the same traditional hand skills are employed as the clockmakers who originally made them, in many cases, nearly 300 years ago.

ADDRESS

5 North Street, Lewes
BN7 2PA

PHONE

01273 473123

WEBSITE

bestofengland.com/186

129

Almond Barn

SHOP | **MAYFIELD** | **TN20 6HX**

The Almond Barn is a 25 year old, fine furniture shop in Five Ashes near Mayfield, specialising in unique wooden furniture and pottery. The barn is also the workshop and home of award winning furniture designer, Charles Thomson who uses local Sussex hardwoods to make his creations by hand.

There are ready-made pieces available from the showroom or, if there is something specific you need, Charles welcomes enquiries regarding personal commissions. His wife Yolande Beer specialises in Japanese inspired pottery, which you can also purchase on-site.

130

ADDRESS

Almond Wood Barn, Mayfield
TN20 6HX

PHONE

01825 830691

WEBSITE

bestofengland.com/161

Borough Wines

SHOP | HASTINGS | TN34 1HT

Borough Wines was born as a small stall on London's Borough market by Muriel Chatel in 2002. Since then Borough Wines has opened seven shops in London, with its eighth in the Sussex town of Hastings. Muriel Chatel comes from a background of wine, with a grandfather who made wine for the French.

There are three hundred types of wines available, yet each one is still hand picked just like day one. The wines often come from smaller producers, helping support the wine industry as a whole. What makes Borough wines that little extra special is Refills, helping you save pennies and help the environment.

ADDRESS

34 Robertson St, Hastings
TN34 1HT

PHONE

01424 434750

WEBSITE

bestofengland.com/160

Freight

SHOP | LEWES | BN7 1XG

Freight is an interesting little shop in Lewes that sells various home ware items, sourced and created within the UK. Their mission is to create own brand products, that represent their own 5 core values; provenance, quality, durability, functionality and exploration.

This is definitely worth a visit if you're in and around Lewes. You will find many original products including soaps, cushions, homemade jams and cups. Such a unique place, you don't want to miss it.

ADDRESS

71 High Street, Lewes
BN7 1XG

PHONE

01273 526123

WEBSITE

bestofengland.com/193

YAK

SHOP | BRIGHTON | BN1 4AD

How about getting creative and joining the crochet community at YAK in Brighton. Everything Yarn and Knitting based is discussed, as well as the latest trends from around the globe. YAK has a fantastic selection of British wools such as Merino from Devon and hand dyed silk from Yorkshire.

They hold regular classes, ranging from how-to-knit jumpers and socks to kids clubs. Instead of buying someone a present, why not go the extra mile and get creative and make one instead. They sell a range of choice patterns to put you to the test.

ADDRESS

16 Gloucester Rd, Brighton
BN1 4AD

PHONE

01273 679726

WEBSITE

bestofengland.com/299

Strand House

SHOP | RYE | TN31 7AY

Strand House Antiques are situated in an historic Grade II Listed, double-fronted landmark Georgian building in the heart of the ancient town of Rye. With exposed brick walls, fireplaces and rustic wooden floors, this carefully curated shop showcases eccentric antiques and playful vintage furnishings.

Its inspiring olde worlde frontage lures you in and features nostalgic designs, from original cherry red Coca Cola fridges to cinematic lighting. Antiqued mirror glass, well-worn leather armchairs and apothecary units are all sourced for inspiration and to add a certain distinctiveness to your interior.

ADDRESS

7 The Deals, Rye
TN31 7AY

PHONE

N/A

WEBSITE

bestofengland.com/302

The Wool Bar

SHOP | WORTHING | BN11 3EG

The Wool Bar in Worthing is an award-winning haven for those that knit, sew and crochet. This relaxing little shop has been providing a warm welcome to locals since 2009 and runs regular knitting themed classes and workshops. They also source and sell vintage, shabby chic furniture.

The owner, Caroline, is passionate about sourcing the best quality yarns from around the world, and is committed to fair trade and ethical buying. If you are looking to learn a new skill, then this is a great place to start.

ADDRESS

2 The Broadway,
Worthing
BN11 3EG

PHONE

01903 235445

134

 bestofengland.com/162

South Down Cellars

SHOP | LINDFIELD | RH16 2HL

South Down Cellars opened its doors for the first time in August 2003. Their founding principle is selling high quality wines and spirits, from the smaller, family-owned vineyards around the world. Knowledgeable and respected staff will guide you through the multitude of choice.

Events are hosted on site and don't always revolve around wine, but also around their spirits collection: the Mad Hatters Gin Party is one of many original events. During your visit, you'll also be able to stock up on some quality nibbles to accompany your tipple of choice.

ADDRESS

70 High St, Lindfield
RH16 2HL

PHONE

01444 484025

135

 bestofengland.com/164

Magazine Brighton

SHOP | BRIGHTON | BN1 4EQ

This very modern and unique shop, Magazine Brighton was a new addition to the Brighton Laines in 2014. They exclusively sell well-crafted, independent magazines. The shop has a database of around 4,000 different magazine titles related to design, the arts, fashion, music, tech, culture and a whole lot more.

Martin Skelton has always been passionate about print, and this is reflected in his shop. It is fantastic to see such creative and unusual prints and the shops wonderful lighting showcases the magazines beautifully.

ADDRESS

22 Trafalgar Street,
Brighton
BN1 4EQ

PHONE

01273 687968

280

bestofengland.com/165

Much Ado Books

SHOP | ALFRISTON | BN26 5UX

Much Ado Books is an award-winning independent shop offering a handpicked selection of new and old books. In 13 years the shop has earned awards and accolades from the national press. Carefully chosen books are thoughtfully displayed over two floors.

Vintage and antiquarian volumes range from Bloomsbury Group rarities to children's books and fiction. The shop's own wonderful notebooks are fashioned from book covers, and there is a tempting range of greeting cards. Events and workshops are also often held in a lovely barn behind the shop.

ADDRESS

8 West Street, Alfriston
BN26 5UX

PHONE

01323 871222

136

bestofengland.com/166

Closet and Botts

SHOP | LEWES | BN7 2NS

Closet and Botts is a partnership between Chloe Shearing and Harriet Maxwell, specialising in vintage, reclaimed and handmade homeware. This eclectic store offers a mix of vintage, new and handmade homeware, furniture and clothes.

The pair spend their weekends crossing the channel to trawl through their secret selection of antique markets in France and beyond. Originally a pharmacy, 196 High Street, with its stained glass windows and tiny walled garden, is a delight.

ADDRESS

196 High Street, Lewes
BN7 2NS

PHONE

01273 945398

137

bestofengland.com/167

Shop @NormanRoad

SHOP | ST LEONARDS | TN38 0EJ

Shop @ Norman Road is a delightful shop and cafe, situated just back from the seafront of St Leonards. This eclectic homeware store is a little gem for finding unique pieces to brighten up your home.

If it's a mug made of bamboo, or some espresso martini chocolate you are after, then this is the joint for you. They also serve a great cup of Joe. Norman Road is full of retro shops and galleries so a great day out for the weekend.

ADDRESS

32 Norman Rd, St
Leonards
TN38 0EJ

PHONE

07763 579908

138

bestofengland.com/168

Seagate

SHOP | HASTINGS | TN34 3EN

Seagate is a classic menswear store in Hastings that focuses on quality British and European clothing brands. Owned by local resident David Whitehill who, wherever possible, promotes local designers and manufacturers that fit the style requirements of his store.

David often makes the scenic journey, up to the bustling streets of London, in order to meet with the owners and designers of the clothing and accessories that he stocks. If you are looking to add a spot of panache to your wardrobe then this is the place for you.

ADDRESS

58 High Street,
Hastings
TN34 3EN

PHONE

01424 532930

139

bestofengland.com/169

Merchant & Mills

SHOP | RYE | TN31 7AT

Merchant and Mills is a small attractive shop, filled to the brim with stylish sewing accessories. Everything is of the finest quality and the majority of the goods are finished with the attractive branding of Merchant and Mills.

The shop itself is relatively small but you're bound to find what you need. Merchant and Mills distribute all over the world and have their merchandise in many of the renowned stylish sewing departments. They have loads of things to look at online, but you should really get to Rye and enjoy the shop.

ADDRESS

14A Tower Street, Rye
TN31 7AT

PHONE

01797 227789

140

bestofengland.com/170

Bluebird Tea Co.

SHOP | BRIGHTON | BN1 1UN

The Bluebird Tea shop is an independent teashop, situated in the heart of Brighton Lanes, specialising in the most creative and flavoursome blends of tea. The staff are expert tea mixologists, so it's safe to say they know a little bit about tea. They have a tea for every occasion.

Their goal is to make people happy with tea. Even if you know nothing about tea, you will when you leave. You're more than likely to find a tea you never knew existed. If you're a big tea lover, its nice to share your passion with others, the small seating area at the back is a great place to relax and chat.

ADDRESS

41 Gardner St, Brighton
BN1 1UN

PHONE

01273 325523

245

bestofengland.com/171

Four Doors

SHOP | RYE | TN31 7JY

Four Doors in Rye is a cheerful little boutique, selling homewares, gifts and stationery as well as work by local makers. They specialise in new & vintage Ladybird books and postcards, but also offer lighting, jewellery and stationery.

An ideal place to spend some time perusing, and finding unique gifts for those who are a little hard to please. It's off the beaten track so well worth seeking out.

ADDRESS

17 East Street, Rye
TN31 7JY

PHONE

01797 223424

141

bestofengland.com/172

Stones Gift Shop

SHOP | ALFRISTON | BN26 5UF

Stones of Alfriston is located in the centre of Alfriston, it has two floors brimming with unusual and quirky gifts. You will find Steiff Bears, Russian Dolls, Glassware, Ceramics and so much more. It is the perfect place to find a meaningful gift for someone special.

The Shop also sells a selection of Sussex ice-cream and sorbets to enjoy on a sunny day. Definitely worth a visit.

ADDRESS

High Street, Alfriston
BN26 5UF

PHONE

01323 871251

142

 bestofengland.com/173

Wickle

SHOP | LEWES | BN7 2LU

In their own words: 'We are a small team of people in Lewes that pride ourselves on offering friendly personal service. We sell an eclectic mix of items for the home and family at fair prices.' This mix includes clothing, gifts, lighting items and lampshades, toiletries, perfumes and toys.

Wickle is where you'll find a map of Lewes on a tea towel at £9.95, wooden lollipops or a train engineer's outfit for a small railway-mad boy. A great place to browse and there's a fantastic tearoom serving teas, coffees and cakes.

ADDRESS

24 High Street, Lewes
BN7 2LU

PHONE

01273 487969

143

 bestofengland.com/174

Flint

SHOP | LEWES | BN7 2DD

A boutique featuring homewear sourced from all over the world, Flint is housed in a 14th Century building in the centre of Lewes. Established in 2002, Flint's ethos, inspired by a love of travel, is to find all sorts of wonderful, unusual and stylish things and carry them home for display and sale.

The collection includes elegant clothes, bags, scarves and shoes complemented by perfumes from brands such as Miller Harris, Jardin d'Ecrivains and Cote Bastide together with natural skincare products. Fresh flowers are available all year round within Flint's floristry service.

ADDRESS

49 High Street, Lewes
BN7 2DD

PHONE

01273 474166

144

bestofengland.com/175

Hutson and Grey

SHOP | CHICHESTER | PO19 1DS

Hutson and Grey is a family run home interiors and gift shop, situated in the town of Chichester. Spread across 4 floors Hutson and Grey offers a huge range of products, all of which are carefully hand-picked. They sell home-ware and gifts, and they are also stockists of Chalk Paint by Annie Sloan.

Meg and Julie were determined to find the perfect business that could be run as a family. It was from there that they went on to open Hutson and Grey in 2014. They also run regular furniture workshops.

ADDRESS

51B South St, Chich-
ester
PO19 1DS

PHONE

01243 696625

145

bestofengland.com/176

Tell us your thoughts.

We want to know what you think of our new pocket guides.

Did we do a good job? Have we missed something? Do you have an idea for how we could improve?

If so, please let us know via our website - bestofengland.com, we would love to hear from you.

Tina Bucknall

HURSTPIERPOINT | BN6 9RE | 01273 831164

Tina Bucknall sell a range of home furnishings, and decorative items. From cake stands, to soft furnishings, you can get everything you need for your home. Stylish, quality and affordable, everything anyone needs.

 bestofengland.com/177

146

Swalk

LINDFIELD | RH16 2HL | 01444 484400

Swalk in the heart of Lindfield is a fine shop selling gifts, Belgian chocolates and cards. The name derives from an acronym used often during the war on letters sent home that stands for "sealed with a loving kiss."

 bestofengland.com/178

147

St Leonards Modern Goods

ST. LEONARDS | TN38 0DS | 01424 718423

St Leonards Modern Goods, was founded in 2010 and has been selling fashion accessories for men and women ever since. They specialise in contemporary leather bags that are handmade by the shop's owner "K". They also stock fountain pens, candles, stationery and socks.

 bestofengland.com/179

148

Paul Clark Clothing

LEWES | BN7 1XG | 01273 474082

Paul Clark offers a broad selection of classic, smart clothes and accessories for the modern gentleman. The shop also sells a range of toiletries and candles. After the success of the men's store he's recently opened a ladies shop a few doors down.

 bestofengland.com/180

149

Wow and Flutter

HASTINGS | TN34 1HG | 01424 439859

Located within the historic America Ground, named for its attitude of freedom and independence, is quirky record and comic store Wow and Flutter. This friendly and welcoming joint joins a thriving hub of shops, cafes, museums and galleries.

 bestofengland.com/181

150

Workshop

BRIGHTON | BN1 1HE | 01273 731340

Workshop is all about simple designs and functionality. The open shop space is full of clean lines, interesting ideas and useful, decorative items. They focus on Lifestyle products and sell a mixture of hanging plants, utilities and bathroom and kitchen items such as chopping boards, knives and crockery.

 bestofengland.com/182

151

Florian

BRIGHTON | BN3 1AF | 01273 328841

Walking along Dyke Road in Hove its hard to miss Florian as the shop and the pavement blend together with a wonderful display of flowers and homeware. Step inside and delight the senses further as the collection of delightful items and colour continues.

 bestofengland.com/183

152

Tom Paine Printing Press

LEWES | BN7 1XU

The Tom Paine Printing Press is the fruition of Peter Chasseaud's project, to set up a working 18th Century style wooden Common Press in Lewes. Located at 151 High Street, it prints artists' and writers' own works, and is also open to the public (10am-5pm Tue-Sat).

 bestofengland.com/184

275

No 1 Antiques

LEWES | BN7 2AH | 01273 477714

No 1 Antiques is a recently opened antique shop in the heart of Lewes with a superbly curated collection of objects for the home and garden. Situated on Cliffe Bridge, this antique shop is owned and operated by a family with over 30 years trading history in Lewes.

 bestofengland.com/185

276

Emmett & White

ALFRISTON | BN26 5UD | 01323 870595

Emmett & White Antiques & Interiors specialise in the wonderful, the unusual and the downright eccentric. They stock pieces ranging from furniture to silver spoons. Emmett & White is a veritable trove of treasures.

 bestofengland.com/297

153

The French Loft

ARUNDEL | BN18 9JP | 01903 882725

The French Loft is a converted barn of antique treasures that is well worth seeking out as it is a great antique shop with a wide range of furniture, lighting and decorative items. French Loft are Specialist Dealers in reclaimed furniture, alluringly arranged over three floors.

 bestofengland.com/189

154

The Clockwork Crow

HASTINGS | TN34 3EE | 01424 716847

The unusual and beautiful to enhance your home and garden'. Clockwork Crow has a passion for curating unique antique pieces in the heart of Hastings Old Town. They also have their very own vegan cafe in-store offering bites in the most interesting setting.

 bestofengland.com/190

155

Bluebelle & Co

BRIGHTON | BN1 4EB | 01273 685026

'A treasure trove of gorgeous gifts' Bluebelle Kids Shop is exactly that. This boutique can be found in the bohemian North Laine shopping district of Brighton. They primarily sell unique children's clothing but have gifts and adults clothing too.

 bestofengland.com/191

156

From Victoria

LEWES | BN7 2NZ | 01273 911415

Victoria Hutchinson is a Lewes based ceramist, who creates beautiful handcrafted porcelain ceramics. She takes her inspiration from the organic forms found in nature – the intricate patterns of coral, the simple form of an unopened flower, the delicate shapes created by the sea and the natural effects of time.

 bestofengland.com/192

157

Harveys Brewery Shop

LEWES | BN7 2AH | 01273 480217

Harveys Brewery shop in Lewes, is within the brewery itself. This family run business is now in its eighth generation, and has been part of the Lewes landscape for over 200 years. The shop offers a great selection of both wines and spirits.

 bestofengland.com/298

122

Eden

BRIGHTON | BN3 3YD | 01273 722030

Just imagine all of your most loved perfumes in one place. Eden match the smells of your favourite brands and create the same scent using botanicals and organic ingredients such as sandalwood, vanilla and jasmine. What's more, all of the perfumes are 100% vegan and haven't been tested on animals.

 bestofengland.com/195

277

CHAPTER FIVE
Food Shops

158

Charlie's Farm Shop

FOOD | PULBOROUGH | RH20 1NP

Charlie Hughes set up his award winning farm shop in 2013 and has built a reputation for his fresh and ethical produce, which is either created on site or sourced locally. The shop is stocked with a seasonal focus, highlighted with wines and beers from popular local vineyards and breweries.

Emphasis is on quality and traceability. All fruit, vegetables, meat and dairy produce are either reared or grown on site or sourced from local, Sussex based farmers and growers. Their butchery serves beef, pork and rose veal which have been reared on the farm and they also have a weekly fish stall.

ADDRESS

Southview Farm, Bury, Pulborough
RH20 1NP

PHONE

01798 303989

WEBSITE

bestofengland.com/197

Sussex Produce Company

FOOD | STEYNING | BN44 3RD

The Sussex Produce Company is nestled in the picturesque High Street of Steyning at the foot of the South Downs. They are both an independent shop and restaurant featuring over 170 of Sussex's highest quality suppliers and have been awarded Best Shop in London and the South East.

The shop stocks an abundance of fresh, local and seasonal produce including breads, cheeses, wines and beers, which you can buy from the barrel to take away. Regular events feature national food authors including Hemsley and Hemsley, Prue Leith and Mary Berry.

ADDRESS
88 High St, Steyning
BN44 3RD

PHONE
01903 815045

WEBSITE
bestofengland.com/196

160

Eggs to Apples

FOOD | HURST GREEN | TN19 7QP

Eggs to Apples is an award winning farm shop and café in Hurst Green. The shop showcases the best of local produce including fruits, vegetables, meats, cheeses, breads and deli treats. Wines, craft beers and spirits are also available with fish arriving daily from Hastings and the South Coast.

There is a café within the shop selling artisan coffee and light bites as well as a garden courtyard. They also host occasional evening events such as tastings and talks to promote food provenance and showcase new products.

ADDRESS

London Rd, Hurst Green, Etchingham
TN19 7QP

PHONE

01580 860566

WEBSITE

bestofengland.com/198

Larder

FOOD | **DITCHLING** | BN6 8UQ

The Larder is a popular local shop and delicatessen located in the heart of Ditchling, providing a curation of local produce. Delicious local cheeses, jams, honey and freshly baked breads are featured alongside an award-winning selection of indulgent cakes and sweeter options.

Filled with great food and friendly people, the Larder has a light and airy interior. Local organic chocolates and wines are also available. Situated at the foot of the South Downs, families often pick up hampers and picnic produce for their weekend walks.

ADDRESS

2 South Street, Ditchling
BN6 8UQ

PHONE

01273 845333

WEBSITE

bestofengland.com/199

Plaw Hatch Farm Shop

FOOD | SHARPTHORNE | RH19 4JL

A 200 acre organic farm on the edge of Ashdown Forest. Their aim is to provide a wide range of biodynamic produce to the local community. Here, they have a dairy herd that provides raw milk, cheeses, yoghurts and cream. There is a large 12 acre garden that provides seasonally available fruit and vegetables.

This is an interesting place to visit, with acres of scenic land and a colourful array of ethically created produce for you to choose from in their farm shop. A 'horsebox cafe' visits every week, serving delicious homebaked goods and hot creamy coffees and teas with milk straight from their herd.

ADDRESS
Plawhatch Lane, Sharpthorne, RH19 4JL

PHONE
01342 810201

WEBSITE
bestofengland.com/200

Hisbe

FOOD | BRIGHTON | BN1 4GU

Hisbe stands for 'How It Should Be'. This passionate and ethical independent supermarket focuses on providing local produce, paying fair prices to suppliers and above living wage to employees. Their mantra is 'happiness before profits' and it's easy to see how Hisbe Organics is achieving this goal.

The spacious store has a wide range of organic and locally sourced goods from meats, dairy, breads, fruits and vegetables to 'planet-friendly' toiletries and even a coffee bar featuring fairtrade coffee. Hisbe prides itself on reducing waste, protecting nature and providing seasonal produce.

ADDRESS

20-21 York Pl, Brighton
BN1 4GU

PHONE

01273 608028

WEBSITE

bestofengland.com/201

Grocer and Grain

FOOD | BRIGHTON | BN1 3PA

You have your mainstream supermarkets and then you have quaint and quirky stores like Grocers and Grain which are great for taking your time and enjoying a brew and slice of cake whilst getting the shopping. Indulgent delicacies tend to get added to your basket alongside healthy grains and an artisanal loaf.

The coffee is well priced and delicious and you can sit outside at one of their many tables and soak up some of Brighton's famous sunshine. Head to Grocer and Grain for all of the obvious and that little bit extra.

ADDRESS

1 Surrey St, Brighton
BN1 3PA

PHONE

01273 823455

WEBSITE

bestofengland.com/202

163

Cowdray Farm Shop

FOOD | MIDHURST | GU29 0AJ

Cowdray is a fascinating estate on the edge of Midhurst and includes an 18 hole championship golf course, the heritage site Cowdray Ruins, the exciting Park Polo Club as well as accommodation, event venues and the popular Cowdray Farm Shop and Cafe.

The Farm Shop has an extensive range of high-end produce with a traditional butchery, a large deli which sells British and continental specialities and homeware. The Cafe serves traditional comfort food and has many freshly made healthy options. There is also a vast courtyard to dine in the sun.

ADDRESS

Cowdray Park, Midhurst
GU29 0AJ

PHONE

01730 815152

WEBSITE

bestofengland.com/310

Hungry Guest

FOOD | **PETWORTH** | **GU28 0AG**

The Hungry Guest food shop in Petworth was founded by Master Baker, Troels Bendix in 2011. They specialise in high quality, locally sourced produce and have a bakery, a butchery, a climate controlled cheese room and a café located on Lombard Street, Petworth.

The interior is a very stylish and welcoming place and they were recently voted Deli of the Year in the Farm Shop & Deli awards 2015. If you are in the area, it is well worth a visit.

ADDRESS

Lombard St, Petworth
GU28 0AG

PHONE

01798 344564

WEBSITE

bestofengland.com/308

Chilley Farm Shop

FOOD | HAILSHAM | BN27 1SE

Chilley Farm has been run by the Plumley family for almost 400 years. The produce sold is of the highest quality and the farm shop has an extensive range of home reared meats alongside fresh fruit, vegetables and free-range eggs. Hot drinks and tasty snacks can be enjoyed next to the cosy wood burner.

Chilley Farm also has a camping area on the site as well as a good play park for children and some farm animals too. Set in a very peaceful location on the Pevensey marshes, it is on the 1066 route from Pevensey Castle to Rye, so if you're out enjoying a walk it's a great place to stop.

ADDRESS

Chilley Farm, Hailsham
BN27 1SE

PHONE

01323 768836

165

 bestofengland.com/203

May's of Stockbridge

FOOD | CHICHESTER | PO19 8QH

May's of Stockbridge's proprietor Vic May is a Master Butcher with experience of over 50 years. Having recently worked for Lord Cowdray's estate, his focus is on the finest quality produce. The best locally sourced meat that Sussex and surrounding Counties can provide is featured in the shop.

With a wealth of experience in traditional and modern butchery, Vic and his team make a wide range of award-winning sausages including Vic's old family recipe for traditional pork sausages and dry cured bacon.

ADDRESS

Stockbridge Place,
Stockbridge Rd,
Chichester
PO19 8QH

PHONE

01243 786843

166

 bestofengland.com/204

Denniker Farm Shop

FOOD | FLETCHING | TN22 3SH

Denniker Farm provides top quality and locally sourced meat from their farm and from selected local suppliers. Free range meat is their focus and their quality appeals to popular local pubs who serve Denniker's produce on their menus. Their small farm shop has a delicatessen style and knowledgeable staff.

The butchery is under the expert control of Graham Smith who continues to prepare top quality meat, including the famous "Fletching Banger" sausage. They are proud to supply both the public and award-winning establishments including The Griffin.

ADDRESS

Ruston Bridge Rd,
Fletching
TN22 3SH

PHONE

01825 722038

167

 bestofengland.com/205

Nick the Butcher

FOOD | HARTFIELD | TN7 4JG

Situated in the heart of Winnie the Pooh country in Hartfield, Nick the Butchers is not to be missed. This family Butchers is brimming with a wide selection of stunning, locally sourced meat, award winning pies, home-made preserves, a delicious bakery and a good selection of cheese.

With welcoming staff and a great knowledge of the produce on offer, Nick the Butchers is well worth a visit for creating the perfect Sunday roast or Summer BBQ. Renowned for its Drunken Lamb and delicious Pies, it reputably serves the best meat in the area.

ADDRESS

Old Crown Farm,
Sackville Lane, Hartfield
TN7 4JG

PHONE

01892 771311

168

 bestofengland.com/206

"Make Good Art."
N. Gaiman

Turner's Pies

FOOD | BOGNOR REGIS | PO21 2BE

Turner's Pies is an award winning, family-run pie shop and bakery that has been running for 25 years and now has two branches in Sussex. This is their original branch located in Bognor Regis and is very popular with the locals with queues often stretching outside the door.

They sell pies in a variety of sizes with their signature pie being the Steak & Stilton, which was awarded England's Best Steak Pie back in 2013. They also sell a selection of artisanal breads, drinks and cakes.

ADDRESS

89 Hawthorn Road,
Bognor Regis
PO21 2BE

PHONE

01243 841511

169

 bestofengland.com/207

Middle House Deli

FOOD | MAYFIELD | TN20 6AB

The Middle House Deli in Mayfield is a friendly, local farm-shop selling fresh vegetables, fruit, fine cheeses, wines and much more. They also make light-lunches for the locals and visitors who are in need of refreshments to take-away.

Middle House Deli is run alongside the Middle House Hotel and Restaurant located on the opposite side of the road. One of the most impressive buildings in Mayfield, it's hard to miss with its full-timbered walls and striking frontage.

ADDRESS

High Street, Mayfield
TN20 6AB

PHONE

01435 872146

170

 bestofengland.com/208

Lodsworth Larder

FOOD | PETWORTH | GU28 9BZ

Lodsworth Larder is a community run, eco friendly village shop, selling a great variety of fresh and local produce in the heart of The South Downs. With the help of local woodsman Ben Law, it was built by his apprentices and volunteers using local materials and was finished in November 2009.

Lodsworth Larder has received recognition for its design and has won many awards. The store is well stocked for a village shop and has everything from fresh groceries and medicine to a postal service. The area is very popular with walkers and cyclists and the Larder is the perfect place to stop.

ADDRESS
The Street, Lodsworth
GU28 9BZ

PHONE
01798 861947

171

bestofengland.com/209

F Richards & Sons

FOOD | LEWES | BN7 1RL

Frank Richards & Sons is a quality local butcher shop, located in Lewes. Opened in 1934 by the Richards Family, the shop has been run through the generations and is now managed by Frank Richards' grandson, who continues the family's philosophy of creating excellent produce.

Selling a range of locally sourced produce, as well as selected meats from around Sussex, they age their meats to ensure you get the fullest flavours when cooked.

ADDRESS
25 Western Rd, Lewes
BN7 1RL

PHONE
01273 473086

172

bestofengland.com/210

The Old Spot

FOOD | PILTDOWN | TN22 3XN

The Old Spot is a popular farm shop full of local and home-made farmhouse produce. Established for over 25 years and family owned, they have a traditional butcher's within the shop specialising in high quality, naturally reared meat and poultry from traceable local farms.

The meat is cut and prepared on site and their bacon is traditionally cured and smoked in their own smoke house. Sussex cheeses, pickles, vegetables and cakes are sold alongside practical country essentials including sacks of firewood.

ADDRESS

Piltdown, Uckfield
TN22 3XN

PHONE

01825 722894

173

bestofengland.com/211

Glyn Thomas & Sons

FOOD | LINDFIELD | RH16 2HL

Located in the heart of Lindfield, Glyn Thomas and Sons Butcher is the traditional, family village butcher that everyone would love to have on their doorstep. Specialising in local meats, much of it farmed on the South Downs, they pride themselves on the traceability and quality of their produce.

The butcher has been voted as one of 'Britain's 50 best foodie addresses' in the Telegraph. With GM free, free range pork, organic beef and home-made delicatessen style produce, it continues to be a favourite shopping destination for locals.

ADDRESS

40 High Street,
Lindfield
RH16 2HL

PHONE

01444 483303

174

bestofengland.com/212

Heals Farm Shop

FOOD | MAYFIELD | TN20 6HL

Heals Farm Shop and Café is a charming new farm shop situated between Five Ashes and the historic Mayfield in East Sussex. This is a popular purveyor of pies, cheeses and local meats. Fresh fish from Newhaven is brought in daily alongside wines and beers from local vineyards and breweries.

Heals works together with Leppard's family butcher of Mayfield to ensure their meat produce comes from happy, well kept animals within the local area. Their cafe also serves generous breakfasts and lunches as well as a popular Sunday roast.

ADDRESS

Mayfield Road, Five
Ashes, Mayfield
TN20 6HL

PHONE

01435 873984

175

 bestofengland.com/213

Middle Farm

FOOD | LEWES | BN8 6LJ

Nestling at the foot of Firle Beacon on the South Downs near Lewes, Middle Farm is a 625 acre working farm that features a popular farm shop, cafe and cider barn. Visitors can taste, compare and buy from a range of over 100 different draught ciders and perries (including the farm's own Pookhill Cider).

With a picnic area, nature trail and two outdoor playgrounds, children can meet playful rabbits and guinea pigs, rare breed chickens, huge pigs, llamas, goats, dairy cows and fluffy sheep. The farm shop sells delicious, locally sourced produce and features home-baked goods, a butchers and cheese counter.

ADDRESS

Firle, Lewes
BN8 6LJ

PHONE

01323 811411

176

 bestofengland.com/214

The Pink Cabbage Produce

MAYFIELD | TN20 6AB | 01435 872557

The Pink Cabbage Produce Co is a fusion of a coffee shop, delicatessen and fine cafe, where you can enjoy freshly ground beans and the finest local ingredients beautifully crafted into delicious dishes. Tumbling out of the shop is a selection of colourful produce, highlighted with pretty flowers and plants.

 bestofengland.com/215

 177

Holmanbridge Farm Shop

LEWES | BN8 4TD | 01273 401964

Holmanbridge farm is family run and provides superb free-range local and British produce in the heart of Sussex. What started with the family selling their fresh eggs at the farm-yard gate, has grown into the successful farm shop they now run.

 bestofengland.com/216

178

Roots Urban Farmshop

EASTBOURNE | BN21 4TJ | 01323 723008

Roots is an urban farmshop, coffee shop and café located in the center of Eastbourne, providing fresh home-cooked food and showcasing a great little farmers market. They use and sell a range of fresh, locally sourced, pesticide free produce alongside home-baked cakes and pastries.

 bestofengland.com/217

179

Cates Delicatessen

PETWORTH | GU28 0AP | 01798 343634

Cates Delicatessen and Cookshop, located in the heart of Petworth is a family run business renowned for its wide range of curated kitchen goods. A deli, cafe and specialist shop, Cates specialises in essential cooking and baking tools, providing customers with unique gift ideas.

bestofengland.com/218

180

CHAPTER SIX
Culture

Ditchling Museum

CULTURE | DITCHLING | BN6 8SP

Situated in the heart of the South Downs within the pretty village of Ditchling, is the award-winning Ditchling Museum of Art + Craft. Witness a fine collection of artwork and artefacts centering on artists who've settled in the area in the early 20th century, alongside a more contemporary programme.

Since the arrival of its artistic inhabitants, Ditchling has been renowned as one of the most important places for visual arts and crafts in Britain. When visiting the museum you can expect to see fine examples of sculpture, wood engraving, print, typography, textiles, calligraphy and much, much more.

ADDRESS
Lodge Hill Lane, Ditchling, Hassocks
BN6 8SP

PHONE
01273 844744

WEBSITE
bestofengland.com/222

182

De La Warr Pavilion

CULTURE | BEXHILL | TN40 1DP

The De La Warr Pavilion in Bexhill-on-Sea has become a modernist icon on the South Coast and provides a fantastic programme of contemporary arts, live music and learning activities. The building was the result of an architectural competition held in 1934 and has similarities to an ocean liner.

As well as browsing through art or watching famous musicians, you can enjoy some delicious food in the stylish Café Bar that overlooks the beautiful coastline. A large veranda gives you the opportunity to dine outside and get that real holiday feeling.

ADDRESS
Marina, Bexhill-on-Sea
TN40 1DP

PHONE
01424 229111

WEBSITE
bestofengland.com/219

The Towner Gallery

CULTURE | EASTBOURNE | BN21 4JJ

The Towner Art Gallery is an award winning contemporary art gallery and museum in Eastbourne. Every summer, they present a major exhibition on an artist who has a strong connection with their collection or location with recent shows including Eric Ravilious, John Piper and Peggy Angus.

The Towner collection now numbers over 4,000 art objects including oil paintings, watercolours, works on paper, etchings, prints, sculpture, wood cuts and ceramic objects and is one of the most significant public art collections in the South East. Entry is free and they also have a café for light refreshments.

ADDRESS
College Rd, Eastbourne
BN21 4JJ

PHONE
01323 434670

WEBSITE
bestofengland.com/220

184

Jerwood Gallery

CULTURE | HASTINGS | TN34 3DW

Jerwood Gallery is a modern building located in the historic old town of Hastings. Home to the Jerwood Collection of modern British art, the gallery also hosts regular, curated exhibitions that celebrate the best of contemporary and British art.

This is no doubt a very interesting and factual place to visit for art fanatics, but it is also suitable for less experienced visitors and families visiting with younger children. There's even a children's trail to help you explore the gallery, its collection and exhibitions.

ADDRESS
Rock-a-Nore Road, Hastings
TN34 3DW

PHONE
01424 728377

WEBSITE
bestofengland.com/221

Farley Farm House

CULTURE | **CHIDDINGLY** | **BN8 6HW**

Farley Farm House is a museum and archive featuring the lives and work of its former residents, the photographer Lee Miller and the surrealist artist Roland Penrose. The house has been beautifully conserved and is full to the brim with surrealist art and sculpture both within the house and throughout the garden.

Farley Farm House is open to the general public for guided tours on certain dates between April and October. Tours are limited to small numbers, so check their website for availability before planning a visit.

ADDRESS
Muddles Green, Chiddingly
BN8 6HW

PHONE
01825 872856

WEBSITE
bestofengland.com/223

185

Chichester Festival Theatre

CULTURE | CHICHESTER | PO19 6AP

Chichester Festival Theatre has been running for over 50 years and is renowned for high quality performances, ranging from large-scale musicals to distinguished dramas. Shows in the past include acclaimed Broadway musicals as well as a number of new plays and classic dramas.

The newly refurbished Theatre reopened in 2014 following a major restoration and upgrade. With this came increased seating capacity, new café areas, bars, an outside terrace and more space in the auditorium for displays of art. The theatre also has a much-valued programme for youth groups

186

ADDRESS
Oaklands Park, Chichester
PO19 6AP

PHONE
01243 781312

WEBSITE
bestofengland.com/224

187

Bentley Motor Museum

CULTURE | HALLAND | BN8 5AF

The Bentley Wildfowl and Motor Museum in Halland is a great day out for everyone. They have a massive range of wildfowl with over 120 species and around 2000 birds. The Motor Museum contains a unique collection of motor vehicles and bikes, a fantastic gathering of stylish and unusual transport.

On site is also a large quiet garden, Bentley Tearooms with delicious cakes and homemade lunches, a miniature railway and plenty of space and playing area's for children to run around. The Bentley site also hosts an annual Wood fair and family festival, with live music and plenty of local ales.

ADDRESS

Harveys Ln, Halland
BN8 5AF

PHONE

01825 840573

WEBSITE

bestofengland.com/225

Charleston

CULTURE | FIRLE | BN8 6LL

Charleston is a property associated with the Bloomsbury Group and was the meeting place for this renowned group of artists and intellectuals. Over the course of 60 years it was also the residence of Vanessa Bell and Duncan Grant and has a fantastic display of some of their most decorative works.

The walls, doors, beams and furniture have all been transformed into a piece of art, taking inspiration from Italian fresco painting and the post-impressionists. The pretty walled garden is also a work of art and is a space to be inspired by. Visit their café and shop after for refreshments and gifts

188

ADDRESS

Firle, Lewes
BN8 6LL

PHONE

01323 811626

WEBSITE

bestofengland.com/227

Zimmer Stewart Gallery

CULTURE | ARUNDEL | BN18 9DG

Zimmer Stewart Gallery in Arundel showcases emerging and established contemporary artists. Work includes contemporary paintings, sculptures, ceramics, textiles and original prints and the gallery holds 6-8 exhibitions each year.

The atmosphere is very relaxed and welcoming. Owners James Stewart and John Zimmer want visitors to feel free to come in and see the work on show, talk about it and feel free to express their honest opinions. A great little gallery, definitely worth a visit.

ADDRESS

29 Tarrant Street,
Arundel
BN18 9DG

PHONE

01903 882063

189

bestofengland.com/226

Driftwood Garden

CULTURE | SEAFORD | BN25 2RD

Set up by Geoff Stonebanks, Driftwood garden in Seaford is only 112ft x 48ft and yet contains a world of delights. The garden follows a sea shore theme with driftwood and bits of boats from the beach used to create a number of different planting areas.

The garden has been open since 2009 and so far they have raised over £50,000 for charity through sales of tickets, home made cakes and teas. Geoff has sold over 4,000 cakes from his garden, quite an achievement.

ADDRESS

4 Marine drive, Seaford
BN25 2RD

PHONE

01323 899296

190

bestofengland.com/228

The Royal Pavilion

CULTURE | BRIGHTON | BN1 1EE

The Royal Pavilion, located in the heart of Brighton, is a must see attraction when visiting the city. Built by John Nash some 200 years ago as a seaside pleasure palace for King George IV, the architecture itself is still visually exciting, with its temple-like spires and oriental twist.

The lawns are generally buzzing in the summer with eccentrics and musicians; making a fine spot for people watching. Inside this majestic building you can learn about its unusual history and see the rooms in their oriental splendour.

ADDRESS

4/5 Pavilion Buildings,
Brighton
BN1 1EE

PHONE

03000 290900

193

 bestofengland.com/229

Pallant House Gallery

CULTURE | CHICHESTER | PO19 1TJ

Pallant House Gallery is located in the historic town of Chichester, tucked away behind East and South Street. In 2006 the Queen Anne House was extended in a bold and exciting style. This gallery holds one of the most significant collections of Modern British Art in the country.

The Gallery doesn't only hold an exciting exhibition programme but it also offers an array of other things to do including talks, workshops for children and adults, tours, a specialist on-site bookshop and an on-site restaurant with courtyard garden.

ADDRESS

9 North Pallant,
Chichester
PO19 1TJ

PHONE

01243 774557

191

 bestofengland.com/231

"Every decently-made object, from a house to a lamp post to a bridge, spoon or egg cup, is not just a piece of 'stuff' but a physical embodiment of human energy, testimony to the magical ability of our species to take raw materials and turn them into things of use, value and beauty. "

K. McCloud

Artichoke Gallery

CULTURE | TICEHURST | TN5 7AE

Based in the attractive village of Ticehurst is the eclectic Artichoke Gallery. In addition to featuring the work of artist/owners Vicki Atkinson, Liz Moys and Louisa Crispin, there are quarterly exhibitions of painting, sculpture, ceramics and jewellery from some of the leading artists and makers around.

The Gallery has a spacious, relaxed atmosphere to show off the contemporary delights on offer, ideal for sourcing that extra special present from highly skilled artisans. Check out the website for a taster but better still, pop in for a sensory treat.

ADDRESS
Church Street, Ticehurst
TN5 7AE

PHONE
01580 200905

192

 bestofengland.com/233

Chichester Cathedral

CULTURE | CHICHESTER | PO19 1PX

Chichester Cathedral has been welcoming visitors through its doors for over 900 years and as entry is free, why not pop in yourself and marvel at its incredible history. The Cathedral is famous for its stunning architecture, which is combined from each century of its life making it both ancient and modern.

They also offer free-guided tours around the site, informing you on the hidden nooks and crannies. Chichester Cathedral is a venue of contrasts from the stunning stained glass to paintings commissioned by Henry VIII to 900 year old ceiling paintings.

ADDRESS
The Royal Chantry, Chichester
PO19 1PX

PHONE
01243 782595

193

 bestofengland.com/235

Anne of Cleves House

CULTURE | LEWES | BN7 1JA

Having received it as part of her divorce settlement with Henry VIII, the irony is that Anne of Cleves herself never visited the beautiful 15th Century Lewes house bearing her name. Today it's home to an excellent museum that includes an exhibition on Sussex iron making and Tudor history.

The garden features traditional plants and employs Tudor-planting methods and they have a decent Café on-site with outdoor seating for the fine weather. Combined admission ticket with Lewes Castle is excellent value. sussexpast.co.uk

ADDRESS

52 Southover High St,
Lewes
BN7 1JA

PHONE

01273 474610

192

 bestofengland.com/237

The Lavender Line

CULTURE | ISFIELD | TN22 5XB

What the Lavender Line lacks in length of track is more than compensated for in a delightful family atmosphere in the heart of Sussex. This preserved stretch of the Lewes – Uckfield rail link that closed in 1969 travels a two mile round trip between the village of Isfield and Worth Halt.

Isfield is the Lavender Line HQ and includes the original Victorian station and signal box. There are two steam and six diesel engines plus carriages; Ivor the Engine is an occasional visitor along with Thomas and special events are held annually from March to October.

ADDRESS

Isfield Station, Isfield
TN22 5XB

PHONE

01825 750515

195

 bestofengland.com/238

CHAPTER SEVEN
Out & About

Rathfinny Wine Estate

OUT & ABOUT | **ALFRISTON** | **BN26 5TU**

Rathfinny Wine Estate is situated on the west side of the wonderful Cuckmere Valley, just three miles from the sea and half a mile south of Alfriston village. The vineyard is 600 acres, with most of the vine slopes enjoying the sun from the south throughout the day.

The vision of the owners, Mark and Sarah Driver, is to create high-quality sparkling wine, in volumes larger than the boutique-scale bottling managed by most English producers. Over the past three years they have planted 72 hectares of vines; by 2020, they will be one of England's largest vineyards.

ADDRESS

White Way, Polegate
BN26 5TU

PHONE

01323 871031

WEBSITE

bestofengland.com/243

Kingscote Estate

OUT & ABOUT | EAST GRINSTEAD | RH19 4LG

The 150-acre Kingscote Estate, is an English wine producer and a venue for weddings, corporate events and private parties. With vineyards, apple orchards and a winery, it produces Kingscote wines and 'cyder'. The shop sells Kingscote products, as well as a wide range of Sussex sparkling wines.

Vineyard tours with wine tasting, clay pigeon shooting and fishing are some of the activities on offer. The 15th century Tithe Barn hosts the cookery school, and is available for hire. Kingscote Estate is set in quintessential Sussex countryside in the Kingscote Valley.

197

ADDRESS
Vowels Lane, East Grinstead
RH19 4LG

PHONE
01342 327535

WEBSITE
bestofengland.com/240

Beachy Head

OUT & ABOUT | EASTBOURNE | SUSSEX

Beachy Head is a stunning spot and is the perfect location to stop and admire the picturesque Sussex Coast. Looking down at the sea from the cliffs is a real eye-opener and the lighthouse in the sea below makes for a great photo.

Walking, running, having a peaceful countryside lunch or a drink at the local pub: this place is a natural beauty that is ideal for all the family. This may not be appreciated if the weather isn't on your side, so make sure the forecast is good before heading out.

ADDRESS
Beachy Head, Eastbourne
Sussex

PHONE
N/A

WEBSITE
bestofengland.com/241

Bolney Estate

OUT & ABOUT | BOLNEY | RH17 5NB

Bolney have been making wine on their Estate since 1972. Since then, they have been recognised on an international stage, to be makers of world class red, white and sparkling wine. The estate remains a family run business by Samantha, the daughter of the owners and founders, Janet and Rodney Pratt.

The estate is 39 acres, and their winery is on site where all the wine is made. There is a café on site, offering gourmet lunches, as well as tastings and tours, on a prebooked basis.

ADDRESS
Foxhole Lane, Bolney
RH17 5NB

PHONE
01444 881575

WEBSITE
bestofengland.com/242

114

Wilderness Woods

OUT & ABOUT | HADLOW DOWN | TN22 4HJ

Wilderness Woods have fantastic grounds and host entertainment for the whole family. The open woodland is great to explore as it's filled with swings, zip wires and hands-on dens for kids. There is a forest school where the kids can learn all about the wild and what it offers.

There is so much space and so many things in Wilderness Woods to explore, that it's bound to open up children's eyes in wonder. The large tarpaulins cover BBQ areas and there is a massive area for large groups and parties. Wilderness Woods also offer an area where you can camp and have a fire.

ADDRESS
Main Road, Hadlow Down
TN22 4HJ

PHONE
01825 830509

WEBSITE
bestofengland.com/244

Arundel Castle

OUT & ABOUT | **ARUNDEL** | **BN18 9AB**

In Norman times, Roger de Montgomery, first Earl of Sussex, built Arundel Castle on a bend of the River Arun to guard a strategic gap through the South Downs. The castle has known three sieges, the last in 1634 by Parliamentarians who were opposed to the rule of King Charles I.

The 'Roundheads' laid it in ruins. Restoration work in the 18th and 19th centuries has made the castle a most evocative and romantic sight. The castle houses a marvellous collection of art including paintings by Van Dyke and Canaletto. Personal possessions of Mary, Queen of Scots are also on display.

ADDRESS
Arundel
BN18 9AB

PHONE
01903 882173

WEBSITE
bestofengland.com/311

201

Firle Beacon

OUT & ABOUT | **FIRLE** |

Firle Beacon sits at 217 metres high and offers incredible views in all directions. The Beacon is situated behind the pretty village of Firle and is partway along the "South Downs Way" which stretches for 100 miles from Eastbourne to Winchester. This particular stretch has some of the best views.

Surprisingly you are able to drive up to this part of the walk, which is fantastic if you are wanting to enjoy the heights without the hike. Paragliders often use this as a jumping point and on a clear day you can see them soaring through the skies. Views out to the sea and inland are unbeatable.

ADDRESS
Firle, Lewes

PHONE
N/A

WEBSITE
bestofengland.com/312

203

East Head

OUT & ABOUT | CHICHESTER | PO20 8AJ

East Head offers a wonderful 6km walk along the sandy beach of West Wittering and around the sand dunes of East Head. There are breathtaking views to be had across to the Isle of Wight and usually kite surfers alongside to entertain.

The beach can get extremely busy in the summer months attracting up to 15,000 people. If you feel like venturing on the walk then take along a bucket and line as the walk passes a popular crabbing pool which local kids adore.

ADDRESS

Coast Guard Lane, Chichester
PO20 8AJ

PHONE

01243 814730

WEBSITE

bestofengland.com/314

The South Downs Way

OUT & ABOUT | EASTBOURNE - | WINCHESTER

Apart from a steep descent into several river valleys, the South Downs Way runs along the top of the rolling hills for no less than 99 miles between Eastbourne and Winchester. Walkers or riders traversing the Way are treated to some of the most spectacular views of the countryside to be found in England.

We are particularly fortunate in East Sussex because access to the South Downs Way is so very easy. You can even drive your car to the top at Devil's Dyke or Ditchling and Firle Beacon and in minutes can be striding out onto South Downs Way.

ADDRESS
N/A

PHONE

WEBSITE
bestofengland.com/315

Bosham Village & Harbour

OUT & ABOUT | BOSHAM | PO18

The quaint attractive town of Bosham is well worth a visit; nestled against the waters edge at the eastern end of Chichester Harbour it's a haven for wildlife and sailing. The small village has an ancient church dating back to the 800's and the small pretty lanes are full of attractive buildings, flowers and character.

There are plenty of places around the area of Bosham for a nice walk. Why not take a stroll around the basin and marvel at the boats and nature, before stopping in one of the village pubs or café's. When visiting Bosham be wary of the tide times as the road and car park flood twice daily.

ADDRESS
Bosham, West Sussex
PO18

PHONE
N/A

WEBSITE
bestofengland.com/261

206

Bluebell Vineyard

OUT & ABOUT | **FLETCHING** | **TN22 3RU**

The Bluebell Vineyard celebrated their 10th birthday last year, and seem to be going from strength to strength. They are located next to the Bluebell Railway and a few minutes drive from Sheffield Park. Their wine growing estate is expanding in size and they have recently opened an on site tasting room.

They run regular tours, so you can find out more about how much time and effort goes into each bottle. We think a trip on the Bluebell Railway followed by a tour of the Bluebell Vineyard, a pub lunch at the Griffin and a walk at Sheffield Park would make a pretty good day out.

ADDRESS
Glenmore Farm, Sliders Lane
TN22 3RU

PHONE
01825 791561

WEBSITE
bestofengland.com/245

Ridgeview Vineyard

OUT & ABOUT | DITCHLING | BN6 8TP

Ridgeview is a family run vineyard, located near the quaint village of Ditchling. Views over the South Downs Ridge give the vineyard its name. Ridgeview pride themselves on producing the highest quality sparkling wines, using traditional methods. They have received multiple awards for their great wine.

The Vineyard is open for tastings and sales throughout the week. They also operate extremely popular tours of their Winery on specific Saturdays throughout the year. The tickets do sell out fast, so book in advance. Ridgeview produce 10 different sparkling wines.

ADDRESS

Fragbarrow Lane, Ditchling Common,
BN6 8TP

PHONE

01444 242040

WEBSITE

bestofengland.com/246

207

Ashburnham Place

OUT & ABOUT | **BATTLE** | TN33 9NF

Ashburnham Place is an English country house, located 5 miles from the town of Battle. It has beautiful grounds, perfect for long countryside walks, with plenty of wildlife and flowers. Ashburnham Place is run by the Christian Trust, however everybody is welcome to visit and enjoy the 220 acres of nature and lakes.

There is a very popular tearoom on site that is well worth a visit, before or after a stroll. If you're religious, or would like a quiet space to reflect in, there are several different prayer rooms and areas where this is possible.

ADDRESS

Ashburnham Place, Battle
TN33 9NF

PHONE

01424 892244

WEBSITE

bestofengland.com/247

East Hill Cliff Railway

OUT & ABOUT | HASTINGS | TN34 3EG

The East Cliff Railways opened on the 10th August 1902, and still retains its original wooden Victorian coaches to this day. It is the steepest funicular railway in the UK and over the years the railway has become a permanent symbol of Hastings unique charm and character.

The East Hill Cliff Railway provides access to Hastings country park via the East Hill for thousands of residents and tourists. The railway also acts as a beautiful vantage point over the town, overlooking the old town and Rock-a-Nore, an area to the east of Hastings.

ADDRESS

Rock-A-Nore Rd, Hastings
TN34 3EG

PHONE

01424 451111

WEBSITE

bestofengland.com/249

209

210

High Beeches

OUT & ABOUT | **HAYWARDS HEATH** | RH17 6HQ

High Beeches is one of the most enchanting gardens in Sussex, they stretch over 27 acres and start high up offering great views over the treetops. You can meander through the wondrous colourful collections of rare plants and sit peacefully by the waters edge.

The gardens are a botanical treasure trove and welcome visitors throughout spring, summer and autumn and there is always something striking either blooming or changing colour to wow the senses. This is a real treat for all ages to enjoy nature and wildlife at its finest and children under 14 get free entry.

ADDRESS

High Beeches Ln, Handcross,
Haywards Heath,
RH17 6HQ

PHONE

01444 400589

WEBSITE

bestofengland.com/250

We have an App for that

Do you want to find the attractions that are nearest to you? Then you need our iPhone app.

The app contains over 250 recommendations throughout Sussex with over 1,000 of our own photos. There's also a handy Google Map for each recommendation.

Visit www.bestofengland.com/app to find out more.

BEST OF ENGLAND
INSPIRING DISCOVERY

Eastbourne Bandstand

EASTBOURNE | BN21 3AD | 01323 410611

Eastbourne bandstand is located directly on the beach front, with open views of the sea. The Bandstand is still thriving, and has over 140 performances and concerts each year. It makes a great place to visit with its unique architecture and picturesque setting.

 bestofengland.com/255

211

The Long Man of Wilmington

WILMINGTON | BN26 5SW

This striking human figure is set in the turf of Windover Hill, on the shoulder of the east side of the Cuckmere Valley. It's clearly visible from the main road between Lewes and Eastbourne. However, due to the constant traffic on the single lane each-way A27, rubbernecking is not advised for drivers.

 bestofengland.com/257

212

Seaford Cliffs

SEAFORD | BN25 1BW

The Seaford Cliffs are a wonderful attraction, even if you don't walk along cliffs, they always look stunning from the coastline. The cliffs provide an amazing walk. You can start at the beach and make your way up a small hill to the top of the cliffs.

 bestofengland.com/258

213

Ouse Valley Viaduct

BALCOMBE | RH17 6QR

Built in 1841, the Ouse Valley Viaduct over the River Ouse on the London-Brighton Railway Line north of Haywards Heath and south of Balcombe is 1,475 feet long. The viaduct was opened in July 1841 and needed 11 million bricks for its construction.

 bestofengland.com/259

214

Tinwood Estate

CHICHESTER | PO18 0NE | 01243 537372

The Tinwood Estate's vineyards are situated at the foot of the South Downs National Park and within walking distance of the Goodwood estate. The estate has been created and is owned by Art Tukker, a charming, Dutch entrepreneur who was born on the farm next door.

 bestofengland.com/248

215

Kingley Vale Nature Reserve

CHICHESTER | PO18 9HR

Kingley Vale is a nature reserve filled with amazing views of ancient trees and long relaxing walks. It is the perfect place to go to enjoy the wonders that nature has to offer. All around there are multiple shades of green broken up by the deep forest browns of the tree trunks and branches that stretch high above you.

 bestofengland.com/262

216

Wey & Arun Canal

BILLINGSHURST | RH14 0RH

The Wey and Arun Canal is a delightful stretch of water that runs 23 miles between London and the South Coast in Sussex. Although much of the Canal is inaccessible and in need of repair, there are still many areas that are very tranquil and well worth a visit. In particular the area around Loxford is a haven for wildlife.

 bestofengland.com/263

217

Heaven Farm

UCKFIELD | TN22 3RG | 01825 790331

Heaven Farm is set in the Heart of the Sussex Weald and has been voted as one of England's most beautiful farms. With 100 acres of attractive parkland it's a great space to walk along the nature trail and indulge in a tasty cake. Heaven Farm have featured on the BBC with their fantastic Bluebell trail, which winds through the woods.

bestofengland.com/264

218

CHAPTER EIGHT
Not to Miss

The Raystede Centre

NOT TO MISS | RINGMER | BN8 5AJ

Raystede is a Sussex based charity that has been admirably looking after and rehoming animals of all varieties for over 60 years. Based in Ringmer near Lewes, they provide sanctuary for over 2,000 animals each year. Entry is free and donations are encouraged to help cover the £6,000 per day costs.

Raystede was founded in 1952 by Miss M Raymonde-Hawkins MBE with the aim of preventing and relieving cruelty to animals and to protect them from unnecessary suffering. Education is an important part of the visit to ensure that children and adults alike know how best to care for their pets.

ADDRESS
The Broyle, Ringmer
BN8 5AJ

PHONE
01825 840252

WEBSITE
bestofengland.com/270

219

Lewes Bonfire Night

NOT TO MISS | LEWES |

Lewes is the Bonfire Capital of the World. Held on the 5th November every year, when 6000 plus residents march through this small town in many different and fantastic costumes.

The Final Procession, the biggest, comes through the centre of town at around 8pm before the six rival Bonfire Societies make for their individual fire sites to toss their torches on the many bonfires and light up the night with spectacular pyrotechnics.

ADDRESS
Lewes

PHONE

WEBSITE
bestofengland.com/278

The Bluebell Railway

NOT TO MISS | HAYWARDS HEATH | TN22 3QL

The Bluebell Railway has no less than 30 engines running on 11 miles of beautifully restored track in the heart of the exquisite Sussex Weald countryside. Vintage buses at the stations provide a wonderful ambience and roaring coal fires in the station waiting rooms transport you to a different age.

You can time your visit to coincide with one of the many themed events held throughout the year from on-board pantomimes to Christmas carols. The passionate staff are knowledgeable about the engines which have been lovingly restored to gleaming perfection.

ADDRESS

Sheffield Park, Haywards Heath
TN22 3QL

PHONE

01825 720800

WEBSITE

bestofengland.com/266

Hunter Gather Cook

NOT TO MISS | LEWES |

Hunter Gather Cook is set just outside of Lewes in beautiful woodlands and offers a unique insight into outdoor living using the natural elements. Run by Nick Weston and his team of experienced bushmen, chefs and outdoor enthusiasts, these courses offer something truly unique.

Hunter Gather Cook offer specialist and seasonal courses which involve butchery of game or fish, foraging walks, fire and wood selection, outdoor cooking and wild cocktail making. They are packed full with information and invaluable techniques that you can use forever.

ADDRESS
1 Barbers Cottage, Beddingham
N/A

PHONE
07921 863768

WEBSITE
bestofengland.com/268

222

Blackberry Farm

NOT TO MISS | **WHITESMITH** | BN8 6JD

Blackberry Farm is set on 18 acres of beautiful Sussex countryside in the little village of Whitesmith. They have a great selection of animals and wildfowl and a good choice of daily activities that are included in the entry fee, such as tractor rides around the farm and animal handling sessions.

Blackberry Farm has a large play park with a huge jumping pillow, swinging boats, assault courses, go-cart tracks and plenty more. The farm is a great day out for the whole family and refreshments are available from their cafe.

223

ADDRESS

Blackberry Farm, Whitesmith
BN8 6JD

PHONE

01825 872912

WEBSITE

bestofengland.com/269

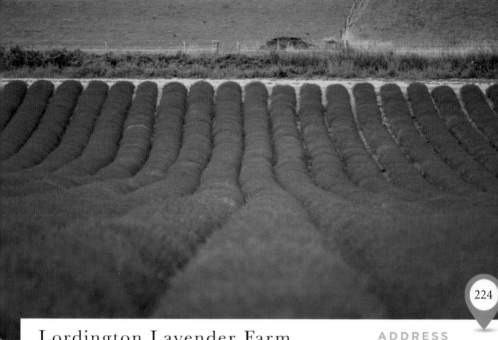

Lordington Lavender Farm

NOT TO MISS | CHICHESTER | PO18 9DX

Lordington Lavender Farm harvests the Maillette Lavender variety, which climbs up the downs, hitting the senses with its vibrant colour and scent. Grown without fertilizers or pesticides, it is a haven for wildlife. During the summer months there is an abundance of rare birds, bees and butterflies.

Each year Lordington Lavender is open for one week in July for visitors to enjoy its mesmerising beauty. It can get very busy, but it is well worth it for the small fee. Homemade cakes and hot drinks are available. Lordington creates and sells a selection of beauty products using their lavender.

ADDRESS

Lordington Farm, Chichester
PO18 9DX

PHONE

01243 378312

WEBSITE

bestofengland.com/271

224

Big Brother is coming

We will be launching a bigger, A4 version of this guide in 2017.

This will have the same lovely content as this guide but will be in an easier to read, coffee table style book.

We think this guide is great for taking out on the road and the A4 guide is ideal for leaving at home and reading on the sofa.

Register via our website to be notified as soon as the book is available.

BEST OF ENGLAND
INSPIRING DISCOVERY

Eastbourne Airshow

NOT TO MISS | **EASTBOURNE** | BN21 3BZ

Eastbourne's International Airshow offers a fantastic display of military fast jets, parachutists, helicopters, incredible aerobatic displays and of course the renowned Red Arrows. The free four-day Airshow has so much to offer and is a great occasion for families, plane enthusiasts and photographers.

Eastbourne comes alive as hundreds and thousands of visitors flock to the beach to watch the amazing aerial performances. On the ground there is plenty of other entertainment, with music, games and lots of eateries. Parking is extremely limited.

ADDRESS
Eastbourne Beach,
BN21 3AD

PHONE
01323 415 415

WEBSITE
bestofengland.com/272

Kino-Teatr

NOT TO MISS | ST LEONARDS | TN38 0EQ

The Kino-Teatr previously known as The Kinema Palace, was opened on 5th November 1913, being the first purpose-built cinema in the town of St.Leonards-on-sea. The building is steeped in history. In 1943 it escaped destruction when it was the target of German bombers.

Although many other buildings nearby were destroyed by German bombings, The Kino-Teatr survived and the current owners have beautifully restored the cinema. This multi-purpose arts centre hosts theatre, live music, films and, on occasion, life-drawing workshops. It is also home to an excellent restaurant.

ADDRESS
43-53 Norman Road, St. Leonards
TN38 0EQ

PHONE
01424 457830

WEBSITE
bestofengland.com/276

226

Goodwood Festival of Speed

NOT TO MISS | CHICHESTER | PO18 OPX

The Goodwood Festival of Speed is an annual hill climb featuring historic motor racing vehicles held in the grounds of Goodwood House. The event attracts the greatest drivers and the rarest, most glamorous cars in the world, both old and new.

The festival is the brainchild of Lord March and has grown into a world-class motoring event which attracts crowds of around 100,000 on each of the three days it is held. If you are a car fan, then there is arguably no greater occassion for you. Tickets sell out well in advance so be sure to get yours early.

ADDRESS

Chichester
PO18 OPX

PHONE

01243 755055

WEBSITE

.bestofengland.com/279

228

Glyndebourne

NOT TO MISS | **LEWES** | BN8 5UU

Glyndebourne is a world-class opera house nestled in the heart of the South Downs. During the summer Festival guests have the chance to get dressed up, enjoy a picnic in the picturesque gardens, and experience one of the six extraordinary operas on stage.

Audiences return to Glyndebourne from October through November to experience three gripping productions before they go out on the road. With shorter intervals, lower priced tickets, and the opportunity to either dress up or dress down, the Tour can have a slightly more relaxed feel. Photo Credit: Clive Barda, Richard Hubert Smith, Sam Stephenson

ADDRESS

New Road, Lewes
BN8 5UU

PHONE

01273 815 000

WEBSITE

bestofengland.com/316

South of England Show

NOT TO MISS | ARDINGLY | RH17 6TL

The South of England Show is a regionally renowned, annual agricultural show held at Ardingly's showground. Showcasing and celebrating the best of the farming industry and country life, it is a feast for the eyes.

There are thousands of animals on display with livestock including dairy and beef cattle, horses, sheep and pigs. The main arena provides entertainment in the form of motorcycle displays and a foxhound parade. The event takes place in June each year.

ADDRESS

Shouth of England Show-
ground, Ardingly,
RH17 6TL

PHONE

01444 892700

WEBSITE

.bestofengland.com/281

CHAPTER NINE
National Trust

230

Sheffield Park and Garden

NATIONAL TRUST | UCKFIELD | TN22 3QX

Sheffield Park has been a recreational retreat since the 18th Century. The beautiful gardens, historical woodland and parkland are a horticultural work of art and nature haven. Diverse wildlife species from Kingfishers to Dragonflies are regularly spotted amongst the vibrant lily pads and colourful flora.

Four lakes form the heart of the garden with meandering paths circulating in and out of the glades and surrounding wooded areas. There are over 87 champion trees planted throughout. Many of them enhance the dazzling autumn colour show that Sheffield Park and Garden is famous for.

ADDRESS
Sheffield Park Gardens,
Uckfield
TN22 3QX

PHONE
01825 790231

WEBSITE
bestofengland.com/283

Bateman's

NATIONAL TRUST | BURWASH | TN19 7DS

Bateman's gives visitors an unrivalled chance to experience what life was like for the renowned author Rudyard Kipling, living and working in the Sussex countryside. The grand Jacobean house was home to the Nobel Prize winning author and poet and his family for over 30 years.

Each room at Bateman's has been left almost untouched. It's as if the Kipling family just popped out for the day. Fascinating treasures from the family's travels are showcased in their natural environment. Rudyard's study boasts an impressive collection of books. ©National Trust Images

ADDRESS
Bateman's Lane, Burwash,
TN19 7DS

PHONE
01435 882302

WEBSITE
bestofengland.com/291

231

Nymans

NATIONAL TRUST | HAYWARDS HEATH | RH17 6EB

The Nymans estate was purchased in the 19th century by Ludwig Messel. In 1915 his son Colonel Leonard Messel succeeded to the property, turning its somewhat humble beginnings into a grand stone manor with over 600 acres of land.

A passion for horticulture is evident at Nymans. Many exotic plants were imported by Ludwig Messel and an extension of the garden was completed by his son. Vibrant summer borders fill the gardens in the warmer months and lush woodlands make for a perfect autumn escape. ©National Trust Images

ADDRESS

Handcross, near Haywards Heath,
RH17 6EB

PHONE

01444 405250

WEBSITE

bestofengland.com/293

Monk's House

NATIONAL TRUST | LEWES | BN7 3HF

Monk's House was the country retreat of Leonard and Virginia Woolf. Bought in 1919, the cottage retains a number of Woolf's personal possessions. With the house regularly hosting the 'Bloomsbury Group' which included T.S Eliot, many of Woolf's finest novels were penned in a lodge in the garden.

Bloomsbury Group members who visited Monk's House included Woolf's sister Vanessa Bell, Duncan Grant, Lytton Strachey, EM Forster, Maynard Keynes and TS Eliot. The garden was a passion and inspiration for the couple and Woolf regularly wrote about its positive impact on her health.

ADDRESS

Rodmell, Lewes
BN7 3HF

PHONE

01273 474760

WEBSITE

bestofengland.com/282

233

Standen House & Garden

NATIONAL TRUST | EAST GRINSTEAD | RH19 4NE

Standen House is a magnificent family home situated in Ashdown Forest and inspired by the Arts & Crafts movement. Designed by architect Philip Webb for the Beale Family, Webb decided to incorporate the medieval farm buildings on the site into his design and drew inspiration from the surrounding landscape.

The house is open to visitors and provides a fascinating look inside the family's country escape. Filled with ornate furnishings and treasures, the family had a passion for the arts. Take a stroll around the tranquil gardens. Image credit - National Trust Images, Chris Lacey, James Masters, Stephanie Rueff

ADDRESS

West Hoathly Road, East Grinstead
RH19 4NE

PHONE

01342 323029

WEBSITE

bestofengland.com/284

The 1st in a series

We are working on a series of travel guides to cover nine additional areas of England.

Each guide will contain hundreds of our carefully selected recommendations and professional photos.

If you want to be notified as to when these are available, please register your email via our website - www.bestofengland.com

BEST OF ENGLAND
INSPIRING DISCOVERY

Petworth

NATIONAL TRUST | PETWORTH | GU28 OAE

Nestled amongst rolling hills and landscaped gardens designed by Capability Brown, stands a magnificent palatial mansion. Petworth House was the southern home for the Percy family, Earls of Northumberland, and remains an impressive piece of historic architecture.

Rooms are adorned by an enviable art collection by world renowned artists including Van Dyck, alongside impressive Classical and Neo-Classical sculptures. Image credit National Trust, Chris Lacey, Andreas Von Einsidel, Arnhel de Serra. ©National Trust Images

ADDRESS

Petworth House and Park,
Petworth,
GU28 0AE

PHONE

01798 342207

WEBSITE

bestofengland.com/285

Bodiam Castle

NATIONAL TRUST | ROBERTSBRIDGE | TN32 5UA

Bodiam, north of Hastings, is now 12 miles from the sea. During the 14th century, when this Medieval castle was built, the River Rother was tidal and the entire valley became an inlet of the English Channel at high water. This moated castle offers guided tours by Medieval characters during the Winter months.

After Bodiam was badly damaged during the English Civil War, 18th-century Sussex eccentric Jack Fuller bought the ruins to preserve them. In 1925 Lord Curzon acquired Bodiam and spent much time and money on having it restored. ©National Trust Images, Esther Ling, Gesine Garz & Trevor Puckett

236

ADDRESS
Bodiam, Robertsbridge
TN32 5UA

PHONE
01580 830196

WEBSITE
bestofengland.com/286

Devil's Dyke

NATIONAL TRUST | **BRIGHTON** | BN1 8YJ

5 miles north of Brighton, Devil's Dyke offers stunning panoramas over the South Downs and impressive views out to sea. Nearly a mile long, the Dyke valley is the longest and widest dry valley in the UK. Legend has it that the Devil dug the dyke to drown the parishioners of the Weald.

The dyke is believed by scientists to have been created during the Ice Age 10,000 years ago. As one of England's most colourful habitats and a haven for diverse insect species, its panoramic view was once described by John Constable as "the grandest view in the world."

ADDRESS
Devils Dyke Rd, Brighton, BN1 8YJ

PHONE
01273 857712

WEBSITE
bestofengland.com/287

Cuckmere Valley

NATIONAL TRUST | SEAFORD | BN26 5TT

Cuckmere Valley is a haven of meadow flowers, rare butterflies and scenic beauty in the lower reaches of the River Cuckmere. This expansive area is known for its picturesque landscape, proving ideal for long walks and even more adventurous pursuits such as paragliding.

Within Cuckmere Valley landmarks include the ancient village of Exceat and the chalk cliffs of Seaford Head. The four villages that make up the Cuckmere Valley parish (Alfriston, Litlington, Lullington and West Dean) are equally charming. ©National Trust Images

237

ADDRESS

BN26 5TT

PHONE

N/A

WEBSITE

bestofengland.com/290

Birling Gap

NATIONAL TRUST | EAST DEAN | BN25 4AD

Birling Gap and its 500 acres of spectacular surrounding open chalk grassland has an abundance of butterflies and delicate downland flowers. Nearby sites of archaeological interest encourage families to walk further along the coast with far stretching views over the water.

Seven former coastguard cottages were built in the 1800s but only four remain due to dramatic sea erosion. As part of the Seven Sisters walk, the cottages and café make a scenic stop-off in between Eastbourne and Seaford with rockpools to keep the kids entertained.

ADDRESS
Birling Gap
BN20 0AB

PHONE
N/A

WEBSITE
bestofengland.com/254

238

238

Seven Sisters

NATIONAL TRUST | EAST DEAN | BN25 4AD

Haven Brow, Short Brow, Rough Brow, Brass Point, Flagstaff Brow, Bailey's Hill and Went Hill; from west to east, these are the very unfeminine names of the Seven Sisters, the pristine white chalk cliffs that lie along the Sussex coast between the River Cuckmere and the dizzying height of Beachy Head.

The undulating path atop the cliffs is part of the South Downs Way and the views are sensational. The wild forces of the sea below create unusual chalk platforms where erosion sees the cliffs retreat by an average of one metre a year. The cliffs and grasslands are home to rare birds. sevensisters.org.uk

ADDRESS
Seven Sisters
BN25 4AD

PHONE
N/A

WEBSITE
bestofengland.com/256

CHAPTER TEN
English Heritage

Pevensey Castle

ENGLISH HERITAGE | PEVENSEY | BN24 5LE

Stretching back over 16 centuries, Pevensey Castle tells the story of Britain's historic fortresses on the South Coast of England. It is here that William the Conqueror landed with his army in 1066.

Steeped in history dating back to the beginning of the 4th century, an exhibition and audio tour details its rich historic relevance and features artefacts from the site. Facilities are limited however there are plenty of picnic areas and open spaces for families and a small shop selling drinks and snacks.

ADDRESS

Castle Rd, Pevensey, BN24 5LE

PHONE

0370 333 1181

WEBSITE

bestofengland.com/292

Battle Abbey

ENGLISH HERITAGE | HASTINGS | TN33 0AD

The Battle of Hastings is one England's most famous battles. It was fought here in 1066 between the Norman-French army of William, the Duke of Normandy, and an English army under the Anglo-Saxon King Harold Godwinson.

Today the ancient battleground is a thriving market town where thousands of visitors come to experience its history each year. English Heritage has made it possible for visitors to follow the course of the battle, visiting important landmarks such as the battlefield and abbey ruins along the way. Photos © English Heritage Trust

ADDRESS

High Street, Battle, TN33 0AD

PHONE

0370 3331181

WEBSITE

bestofengland.com/294

Boxgrove Priory

ENGLISH HERITAGE | BOXGROVE | PO18 0ED

242

Founded in 1117 by the Lord of Halnaker, Boxgrove Priory began with a community of just three monks. Today, the remains of the Boxgrove Abbey are evocative of the past; conjuring images of what life could have been like in the English Catholic Church that began in the 12th Century.

The site is beautiful and English Heritage has kept it in fantastic condition. It is well worth a visit for history lovers. Photos © English Heritage Trust

ADDRESS
Boxgrove
PO18 0ED

PHONE
01243 774045

WEBSITE
bestofengland.com/295

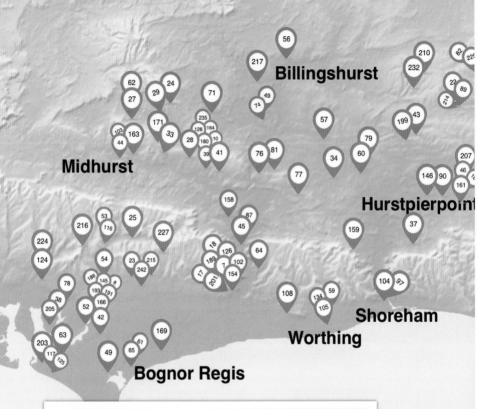

Billingshurst

Midhurst

Hurstpierpoint

Shoreham

Worthing

Bognor Regis

Brighton & Hove